THE SPRING VOYAGE

THE SPRING VOYAGE

The Jerusalem Pilgrimage in 1458

R. J. Mitchell

READERS UNION
JOHN MURRAY LTD
London 1965

This RU edition was produced in 1965 for sale to its members only by Readers Union Ltd at Aldine House, 10-13 Bedford Street, London W.C.2 and at Letchworth Garden City, Herts. Full details of membership may be obtained from our London address. The book is set in 12 point Caslon type leaded and has been reprinted by Camelot Press Ltd, Southampton. It was first published by John Murray.

FOR
ALAN & ANDREW

CONTENTS

1	Introduction	15
2	The Pilgrims	29
3	Venice	47
4	Adriatic Voyage	60
5	The Island of Rhodes	75
6	Cyprus to the Holy Land	83
7	In and About Jerusalem	96
8	The Holy Sepulchre	104
9	Bethlehem	112
10	The Short Way Home	118
11	'The Captain's Business'	124
12	Desert Journey	131
13	Mount Sinai	144
14	Cairo	151
15	Homeward Bound	162
16	Landfall	175
	Appendices	185
	Select Bibliography	191
	Notes	196
	Index	209

ILLUSTRATIONS

between pages 109 and 110

Sketch map of the Voyages

between pages 140 and 141

Portraits of three pilgrims.

Giovanni Martino de Ferrariis. Miniature from a Paris MS. (Bibliothèque Nationale)

Roberto da Sanseverino, from a medal (British Museum)

John Tiptoft, Earl of Worcester. Monument in Ely Cathedral (Photo: Arthur Gardner)

Venice, *c.* 1400, from *Li Livres du graunt Caam* by Marco Polo (MS. Bodley)

Storm at Sea: St. Nicholas calming the tempest by Lorenzo di Bicci (Ashmolean Museum)

William Wey's Map (detail) (MS. Bodley)

The Holy Sepulchre, from a presentation copy of Capodilista's account of this pilgrimage (From *Libri Insigni*. Hoepli, Milan)

St. Catherine's Chapel on Mount Sinai from the *Pilgrim Book* of Gabriel Muffel (Egerton MS.; British Museum)

The Giraffe, from the *Pilgrim Book* of Gabriel Muffel (Egerton MS.; British Museum)

ACKNOWLEDGEMENTS

This is a simple story, told directly from the diaries of those who took part in the spring voyage to Jerusalem in the year 1458; it has, nevertheless, been the occasion for prolonged research that could never have been carried out without the generous help that I have received from many quarters.

First of all I must thank the Council and Fellows of Lady Margaret Hall, Oxford, for electing me to the Susette Taylor Travelling Fellowship for 1963. This has enabled me to travel to Italy in search of further material to add to the researches already financed by a grant from the British Academy. I am deeply grateful for their generosity, and no less for their encouragement.

The President and Council of the British Archaeological Association have very kindly given me permission to reprint some sentences from the paper I wrote on Roberto da Sanseverino in 1938, for which they awarded me the Reginald Taylor Essay Prize for that year. I would like to thank the Association for encouraging my first steps in following the pilgrims from Milan to Mount Sinai. I wish to acknowledge also the courtesy of Professore Paolo Sambin of the Museo Civico at Padua in allowing me to reprint material from an article in his *Bollettino*, and to thank the Editors of *Italian Studies* and *Aurea Parma* for the same kind offices.

For permission to reproduce various illustrations I am indebted to the Trustees of the British Museum, the Ashmolean Museum and the Bodley Library. Also to the Libreria Antiquaria Hoepli, Milan for the picture of the Holy Sepulchre, and to my cousin Mr. Arthur Gardner,

F.R.S.A. for the use of his photograph of John Tiptoft's monument.

Among hosts of helpers in both England and Italy I must offer special thanks to the staff of the Bodleian Library at Oxford, where my studies for this book began and were completed, also to the Department of MSS. in the British Museum. I also wish to thank in particular my old friends Professore Giuseppe Billanovich of Milan, and Professore Giorgio Cencetti, formerly of Bologna, for help spread over many years, also the Direttrice of the Biblioteca Trivulziana at Milan, dottoressa Caterina Santoro, and Dr. Elisabeth Pellegrin of Paris for much practical assistance. I would never have been able to find my way through the maze of archives at Venice without the guidance of dottoressa Tiepolo; I would like to thank her and Dr. Giorgio Ferrari of the Biblioteca Marciana for their patient assistance, also dottore Fausto Razzetti of Parma for his unfailing help and enthusiasm.

My friend Mrs. Helen Truesdell Heath has spent endless time helping me to phrase and re-phrase the whole book; I am deeply indebted to her for her advice, as I am to Mrs. Ivanka Leader Williams for help in unravelling the meaning of difficult passages in the diaries. Lastly, it gives me pleasure to acknowledge the faithfulness and accuracy of my friend and typist, Mrs. Gertrude Young, who has saved me from many blunders, and the endurance of my family, spread over a long period.

Oxford: 1963

INTRODUCTION

I

From the earliest days of Christianity the desire to make
pilgrimage proved compulsive. The wish to tread where
Jesus and His disciples had walked, and to see and touch
objects associated with them or with the saints and martyrs
of the early Church, was simple and natural. Most pilgrims
found comfort and reassurance, as well as a quickening
of their religious beliefs, through visiting shrines made
sacred by tradition. As one of them wrote on the first page
of his travel diary, it was as important for him as a Christian
to see with his own eyes the Holy Places of Jerusalem
as it was for St. Thomas to examine personally his Saviour's
wounds before he could believe in the Resurrection.

Motives of piety were blended with curiosity and a
lively desire to see the world. It is sometimes forgotten that
in medieval times most laymen, as well as the great majority
of clerics, led extraordinarily static and insipid lives. For
people whose existence was circumscribed by convent walls
or parish boundaries a pilgrimage was a wonderful opportunity to extend their horizon. Members of religious com-
munities might sometimes be given leave to study in foreign
universities, or be sent on business to the Roman Curia,
but to be chosen as a representative to make a pilgrimage
in order to gain indulgences for one's brethren, or to secure
holy relics for one's church, was a rare privilege. Ordinary
men and women, too, of all ages and from every walk of
life, faced the rigours and hardships without flinching,
indeed, with every sign of pleasure. They were upheld,

no doubt, by their idealism, but there was also in most
pilgrims a strong streak of the tourist.

For many years the Crusades had provided adventurous
careers for those who found little scope for their ambition
in a dull provincial life, or who were bored with the
formalism of jousts and tourneys. When at last this movement lost its impetus, pilgrimage to distant shores seemed
the best substitute. Thus, the ranks of sober pilgrims were
swelled by unarmed soldiers of fortune wearing the cross
instead of the flamboyant badges of chivalry they had
sported in an earlier age.

There was in any body of pilgrims far less distinction
between rich and poor than there was divergence of character between individuals. The rich and self-important might
secure for themselves better amenities on board ship, but
as soon as they reached the Holy Land they had to
learn that there one pilgrim was as good as another.
Sharing danger and adversity—as always—brought out
unsuspected qualities of patience, endurance, and humour,
as surely as it showed up selfishness or craven fear. There
were, of course, excellent reasons for fear of the unknown
hazards; any pilgrim with normal imagination had to face
the possibility that he might never return. Only the very
casual or very stupid traveller failed to make his will before
he left home, although it was possible to defer the task until
he reached Venice, where special facilities were arranged
by the Senate whereby lawyers, scribes, and even witnesses
could be supplied at a moment's notice.[1]

Even those who could not themselves take part in a
pilgrimage were able to enjoy it vicariously. Pilgrims
setting out on their travels were customarily seen off on
their journey by a great crowd of their fellows, who felt that
through helping the pious intention they themselves shared
in the virtue of the exercise. Sometimes the town band
would turn out to cheer them on the first mile or two of their
journey, and church bells were often rung to mark the

pilgrims' departure. Along with the gifts and garlands showered upon them by their friends, the pilgrims knew that they had the good wishes and prayers of the whole community to sustain them in darker moments. When that determined globe-trotter Margery Kempe planned her journey to Palestine in 1436 the Bishop of Lincoln not only gave her permission and encouragement,* but added a present of twenty-six shillings and eight pence "to buy her clothes with, and to pray for him".[2]

The return home was quite another matter. For one thing, it was seldom possible to forecast the exact day of arrival. Pilgrims who had set out in a group were likely to come home in ones or twos as their circumstances dictated. Naturally there were warm family reunions, relations and friends gathering to welcome the travellers and to listen patiently to their experiences. It may be supposed that the tales they had to tell were already familiar: by the mid-fifteenth century pilgrims had been visiting Jerusalem for something like a thousand years, so it cannot have been easy to find anything fresh to say. The hardships and the wonders of the journey were real enough to the travellers; it must have been a temptation to dwell upon them at inordinate length.

This tendency was deplored by a Milanese knight,[3] who criticized his fellows for their boastfulness. "A man should undertake this voyage," he wrote, "solely with the intention of visiting, contemplating and adoring the most Holy Mysteries, with great effusion of tears, in order that Jesus may graciously pardon his sins; and not with the intention of seeing the world, or from ambition, or to be able to say 'I have been there' or 'I have seen that' in order to be exalted by his fellow men." The knight's standards were perhaps too high; he did not make enough allowance for human nature. It was, indeed, a natural thing for pilgrims to wish to share

* Her absence from home may have brought some relief to the diocese, as it certainly did to her long-suffering husband.

their experience with the stay-at-homes; even the most devout could scarcely be expected to keep such an overwhelming experience to himself. If pilgrims had not spoken or written of their travels, posterity would have been the poorer. That certain diaries chance to have survived, where so much literature has been lost, is a happy accident for those who like to discover how their forefathers lived and what they thought about the world they lived in. It is astonishing to find how 'modern' were some of their reactions.

II

In the course of centuries a mass of pilgrim lore had been accumulated; constantly it was amended, brought up to date, discarded, rediscovered. Those who set out advice and information for their fellows drew freely from the common stock of legend and experience, without any more thought of plagiarism than the physicians who tabulated wisdom from the ancients, or cooks who set down recipes gathered from their grandmothers. Plagiarism was not a dirty word in the fifteenth century, for it had no meaning at all. Writers of guide-books sometimes considered a particular public, as the Scottish composer of an itinerary on conventional lines who devised an extension from Dover to Edinburgh,[4] or they might include some useful piece of information that had just come to hand, or an anecdote that they had lately heard. A university professor took the trouble to write his *Flowers of the Holy Land*[5] in the vernacular, "so that it may be read by the unlearned"; he must have expected to attract a large number of less educated readers.

Some of these guide-books are colourless to modern readers, but that does not mean that they were not useful in their generation. They existed, of course, in manuscript; there is a suggestion, however, that they must have been widely circulated, judging by the astonishingly large number that were issued by the early presses at the end of the century, in Europe and even in backward England, where the *Information for Pilgrims unto the Holy Land* ran through several editions. This was probably written by 'Master Larkes'[6] but careful examination shows that the author copied much of it word for word from a description dated at least two decades earlier. The model for the *Information* is, indeed, the book written by one of the pilgrims in 1458, the Englishman William Wey. His *Itineraries*,[7] although of course the material is largely drawn from earlier sources, is strikingly original in its arrangement and in the scope of its advice to would-be pilgrims. By the mid-fifteenth century most people were familiar with the 'aids' that were available; it was, however, important for pilgrims to have short and precise notes of the best route for their personal needs. It was for an English public travelling in an orthodox and economical manner that Wey wrote his book.

In his proem to the *Itineraries* William Wey adds to the valuable instructions for shopping, and for making one's covenant with the *patrono* of a pilgrim galley for a 'package tour', full information about the changing of money. Even today travellers find difficulty in working out comparative rates of exchange; in the later middle ages it was a still more complicated problem. It seems that William Wey was the first writer to tackle this matter seriously: he showed himself to be a knowledgeable guide. Coins varied in value from town to town; a Venetian ducat, for example, was always worth more than a Roman one, but it was worth less in Cyprus than in Rhodes. It would seem that the value diminished as the distance from Venice increased. Wey warned his readers against accumulating too many local coins, "for they laste but lytyll way, there be so many dyvers chaunges of them in dyuerse lordshyppes, and [those] . . . of the one lordshyp woll not goo in the next lordshyp".

The same qualities that characterize Wey's *Itineraries* are seen also in the map that he drew to illustrate them. This is assumed by general consent to be the one now in the

Bodleian Library[8] that was printed in Wey's name more than a hundred years ago by the Roxburghe Club. It is not signed, nor is any indication given of its provenance, but notes of distance between towns, and the place-names, are practically identical with those in the *Itineraries*. Many details, too, agree closely with Wey's own explanation of his map. Here, as in the book, Wey may well have drawn upon accumulated stores of knowledge.

It would be foolish to compare Wey's map with the geographically far more correct *portolani* or sailors' charts of the mid-fifteenth century, for they were intended for an entirely different purpose. Indeed, these bore no more relation to picture-maps than do sheets of the Ordnance Survey to the modern 'Routes' drawn up by a tourist agency. Wey's masterpiece is seven feet long and sixteen and a half inches wide. It begins on the left, that is, North, with Damascus. It extends to Beersheba, the lower edge showing the sea coast from Sidon to Gaza. Not only does Wey give the names of the chief cities in very recognizable spelling, he represents also famous sites and buildings. Sometimes he tries to indicate biblical stories by drawings —for instance, six stone water pots mark the position of Cana of Galilee. It may be noted that he avoids the common error of confusing Caesarea the coastal town with Caesarea Philippi in Galilee. The colours of Wey's map are clear and bright; towers are neatly striped in red and blue, roofs are shingled with blue tiles. He does not waste space or distract the eye by including grotesques or imaginary or traditional beasts, although there are birds in the trees of Mount Lebanon, red and white rabbits on the plains, and a variety of fish—including pike and eels—in the Sea of Galilee. Mountains and plains are green, lakes and rivers a strong blue; the Dead Sea is sufficiently transparent to show the submerged Cities of the Plain.

The most emphatic of Wey's admonitions—as, indeed, of all writers on pilgrimage—was the necessity for securing a licence that would act as a rudimentary passport. The numbers of those making pilgrimage overseas would have been even greater than it was, had all those who wished to travel been able to do so without formality. But the last word was with the Pope, from whom the licence must be obtained, although he often delegated this power to the bishops. The theory was that only through Papal permission could Christians be allowed to pay dues that would go to the Muslim community and so "swell the coffers of antichrist". It is easy to understand the warning given by several experienced travellers to their fellow pilgrims that three sacks would be necessary for this expedition—one filled with necessities (food and clothes), one with patience, and one with money. "But the largest of these must be the money-bag."[9]

III

The year 1458 saw continued ferment in eastern Europe, where the provinces* of Hungary and Bosnia were desperately resisting the advance of the Ottoman Turks, based as they now were upon Constantinople.

Five years earlier the capture of Constantinople by the Ottoman Turks, under their brave leader Mahomet II, had shocked and horrified the whole of Christendom. Aeneas Sylvius Piccolomini, afterwards Pope Pius II, was voicing public opinion when he said the fall of this citadel was a "great scandal to the Christian religion".[10] He also wrote to the reigning Pope that of the two lights of Christendom one had been put out.[11] Yet the news should have taken no one by surprise. Sixty years had passed since a great army of crusaders had been routed at Nicopolis by a smaller Turkish force that was better organized and very much better led. At the time and afterwards, in the face of the plainest evidence, western Europeans had refused to accept

* Of the Holy Roman Empire.

the fact of their defeat. They continued, ostrich-like, to bury their heads in the sand of delusion, believing that their ineffective catapults could match Turkish artillery from the world-famous arsenal of Adrianople. As recently as 1444 Christian troops had met a humiliating defeat at the battle of Varna through under-estimating the quality of the Turkish bowmen; this was little more than a skirmish, but it showed that the crusaders had learned nothing and forgotten everything.

The state of the chief nations of Europe was a formidable obstacle to unity. Germany was no more than a collection of provinces and bishoprics, animated chiefly by jealousy and rancour, under an Emperor who scarcely amounted to a figurehead. France, Burgundy, and England were entangled in the aftermath of their senseless wars: England torn by civil strife, France trying hard to repair her fortunes, and Burgundy intent upon reviving—if she could—the middle kingdom between France and Germany that had existed only as a memory since the days of Charlemagne's son Lothair. As Aeneas Sylvius Piccolomini wrote in his *Commentarii*,[12] "France had been worn down by so many misfortunes that she presented the appearance less of a kingdom than of a desert waste." Only in Italy were matters deceptively quiet; the Peace of Lodi in 1454 had given a breathing space to the chief states, but private, piecemeal, wars still smouldered while the mercenary captains, the *condottieri*, looked keenly for employment that was seldom difficult to find.

In such conditions it is not surprising that the number of European pilgrims had dwindled throughout the century. Few now made their way from Iceland and Scandinavia across central Europe, where they might so easily become involved in faction fights even if they did not fall a prey to robbers, floods, or avalanches, in unfriendly mountain country. Many English pilgrims were ready to settle for the shorter journey to Compostella in northern Spain, rather than face the expensive and hazardous Jerusalem expedition. The little ships from Bristol and Southampton, scudding across the Bay of Biscay, gained the passengers who a hundred years earlier would have crowded the Venetian galleys, but the Venetian captains meticulously kept up their high standard of service in the hope of tempting back the pilgrim traffic.

Venice was largely dependent upon her Levantine trade; she had no intention of falling out with her best customers, the Ottoman Turks. The other major power in North Italy was the Duchy of Milan; her Duke saw clearly that he would be expected to take the lead in opposing the Turkish advances towards Albania and the Gulf of Trieste. Like the wise man he was, Duke Francesco Sforza intended to make no move until he had accurate information about the problem that faced him. Sforza wished to collect facts and opinions concerning the Eastern rulers, so that he could estimate their strength and their ambitions, together with the dependability of their allies. For this reason he had appointed envoys to Alexandria* a few years earlier, and with the same end in view he planned to send his own nephew to Palestine in 1458, in the guise of a pilgrim, to try to find out all that he could about the Turkish advance and the most likely direction of the next attack. Sforza's nephew, Roberto da Sanseverino, was ready enough to make the pilgrimage and to try his hand at diplomatic activity, although in the end the pilgrim took charge of the diplomat. He wrote his uncle three letters,[13] short bulletins or progress reports rather than formal despatches; Sforza cannot have gleaned very much information from them.†

* Corrado da Fogliano and Giovanni Matteo Butigella: See Chapter 2.

† The most precise is the one now in the State Archives at Milan. (The others are in Paris.) "Since your Excellency is desirous of learning about the progress the Turks are making," he wrote, "we have been told by their merchants that the army is spread round a large city called Salonika and that it numbers more than a hundred thousand and is well furnished with munitions and other necessities for the campaign."

Introduction

It should be made clear that whereas the Ottoman Turks were pushing their way into Europe during the middle years of the fifteenth century, they did not secure control of the Holy Land until 1511. At the time of the pilgrimage in 1458, Palestine was occupied by their kinsmen, descended from those Turks who had recaptured Jerusalem from the Crusaders in 1187. The country was administered by the Mamluks whose background and activities are outlined in a later chapter.* Far from resenting the visits of pilgrims —so long as they behaved themselves becomingly—the Muslims were glad to welcome them to Palestine. The provision of guides and the imposition of tolls not only ensured that the pilgrims kept to the beaten track, it also helped the exchequer. The sale to these tourists of mass-produced reproductions of the Holy Sepulchre and other such souvenirs was one of the more important sources of revenue. Still more lucrative was the traffic in "the earth from which God fashioned Adam". The Saracens used to dig this in large quantities, loading the precious soil into crates and exporting it not only throughout Europe but also to Egypt, Ethiopia and the Indies. The supply was virtually inexhaustible; it was said that the pits whence the earth was taken filled themselves again, mysteriously, within the course of a year "without any castings in or helpe of mannes hande". This earth was treasured not only as a relic but also as a safeguard against epilepsy.

Besides trading with the pilgrims in these recognized

---

* The pilgrims remained unaware of any distinction between the terms 'Governor', 'Khalif', or 'Emir' (often rendered as 'Admiral'). Any such official ruler might be described as 'Sultan'. Where following this usage does not do actual violence to the meaning, this practice has been followed: to lessen the confusion I have preferred to write 'Muslim' rather than Turk. Similarly, since this book is addressed to the intelligent general reader rather than to specialists, I have chosen the more familiar and popular forms of expression. Thus, names are spelled as the pilgrims wrote them rather than in their more correct form—'Syon' instead of Zion, for instance, and 'Mahomet' for Muhammad.

ways, the Muslims derived a steady income from the tolls and tributes that they exacted from them. These were mostly fixed by custom, but individual pilgrims were sometimes subjected to petty extortion in the form of illegal tolls. The obviously rich men were, of course, much more liable to this treatment than the poor and humble. Muslim officials were very particular about writing down each pilgrim's name and status in their records, although their diligence might be thwarted by the aristocratic pilgrims' habit of assuming shabby clothing. On the whole the officials were fair and honest; the complaints against their rapacious demands generally came from pilgrims who resented having to pay anything at all for the privileges they required. Occasionally there was a black sheep, like the officer in charge of one party, who asked for illegal tribute. He had misjudged the temper of these pilgrims, for they fell upon the Muslims, over-powered them, and carried them before the Governor of Jerusalem, demanding justice. "The Governor," wrote one of them in his diary, "at once held his inquiry and pronounced sentence of death on the officer, whose head was cut off without more ado."[14]

Very few pilgrims took such direct action: when they were faced with what they thought to be extortionate demands they remembered the maxim: 'on a pilgrimage the mouth of your purse must always be open'. They grumbled, but they paid, contenting themselves with des-cribing the Saracens as 'avaricious', or 'ribald', or 'malicious', or referring to their Palestinian hosts as 'those Saracen dogs'. Even William Wey, normally so temperate, remarked: "The Sarsenes wyl go talkyng wyth yow and make goyd chere, but thay wyl stele fro yow that ye have an they may."

The word 'Saracen' was really an inheritance from the Crusades, a term that was used very loosely, denoting noth-ing more than 'easterner'.* Although the reference was

* The term came into use in the third century. The Latin 'saracenus' is from the Arabic 'shargi', meaning east.

usually to Turks, it might cover Muslims of many races, whether Moors, Arabs, or Bedouin, or even the ancient Christian community of Copts, or 'Christians of the Girdle'.* 'Saracen' is an unscientific term, but convenient where it is used in the sense of 'non-European', the meaning that it conveyed to the pilgrims of 1458. For the sake of simplification it is used here in the same way.

Although they were aware of the great racial differences pilgrims easily became confused by the variety of languages they heard spoken around them; during their short stay in Palestine it was hardly possible to differentiate between the civilizations that surrounded them. To Europeans, all dwellers in Syria, Palestine or Egypt were 'Saracens' whether or no they added as a matter of form that they were 'dogs' or 'thieves'.

Even liberal-minded pilgrims mentioned the Saracens in a denigrating style, rather because it was the general convention than from a desire to express any real indignation at their behaviour. In actual fact, both sides showed considerable tolerance: the Muslims treating the pilgrims with consideration and courtesy when they might well have exploited their inexperience, while the pilgrims for their part genuinely tried to respect what they looked upon as strange prejudices. When they offended, it was usually through ignorance rather than from arrogance. This civility was reciprocated as a matter of policy; it is significant of both points of view that when a Muslim military mission came to Venice in 1482 its members were received cordially and with high honour, being awarded their own place in the

* In his *Viaggio* Roberto da Sanseverino defines these as: "so-called because their ancestors were converted by miracles performed by St. Thomas the Apostle with the girdle of the glorious Virgin Mary, that he received from her when she ascended into Heaven. In memory of this, and as a sign of devotion, whenever they enter a church for worship, these Christians tie on a girdle made just like those that are sold for the measure of the Holy Sepulchre. It is said that the girdle they wear is a replica of that belonging to the glorious Virgin." They were also known as Jacobites.

Corpus Christi procession—to the consternation of a visiting German friar* who regarded them as "dogs, and right enemies of the Sacrament".[15]

The growth in strength and the spread of Islam was becoming more and more significant to eastern Europe.[16] As time passed it grew increasingly clear that the West must come to terms with the Muslims, whether by force of arms in yet another Crusade, or by co-operation. The way to this second alternative had already been pointed by the efforts of Venetian and other traders, whereby Levantine and Syrian goods flowed increasingly into European markets. When Cardinal Nicholas of Cusa† drew up plans for a conference between East and West[17] he suggested that merchants from Cairo, Alexandria, and Asia Minor should attend in order to describe "at first hand the ideas and practices of Islam. And when materials had been collected, he wanted to have intermediaries sent from the West to Islamic countries, preferably, he says, temporal princes whom the Turks prefer to priests."[18]

The same Nicholas of Cusa wrote a commentary on the *Koran*; he was greatly preoccupied with the idea of unity and was continually seeking for points of contact rather than differences between Christians and Muslims. Similarly, Pope Pius II could see no reason why the Sultan Mahomet II should not dissolve all conflict by the simple expedient of accepting Christian baptism. It would require, as the Pope pointed out in his famous *Letter*,‡[19] only the exercise of goodwill and the provision of a small quantity of water. There was nothing cynical about the Pope's attitude; he was perfectly sincere. The *Letter*, indeed, is a masterpiece of persuasive argument. Professor Southern calls it a "magnificent composition", commending its splendour of

* Brother Paul Walther, a Franciscan from Heidelberg.

† He died in 1464, worn out by strife and disappointment in his efforts to promote unity.

‡ Written, almost certainly, in 1460.

27

language and its worldly wisdom.[20] Unfortunately for the cause of peace, this epistle had more effect in the Western world than in the East; it is doubtful if it ever reached the eyes of the Sultan. One thing emerges, however. That is that a liberal and tolerant spirit existed in both camps, something quite new and extremely important to future generations.

The fall of Constantinople to the Ottoman Turks in 1453 had brought the whole matter sharply into focus. Academic discussion was no good when the enemy was hammering at the gates. Military-minded die-hards at once began to fumble for the ancient weapons—a Crusade! a Crusade! they cried. Even Pope Pius II, who wrote so rational a letter to the Sultan, wore himself out in the effort to collect men and supplies for the forlorn expedition that he hoped to lead. Some paid lip-service to the idea; they subscribed to the project of a Crusade without proposing themselves to take any active role. But for the most part people preferred to look upon Levantines and Syrians less as natural enemies than as potential customers. To members of the pilgrim party in 1458 it was no longer a new idea that Muslims could be men not only of the same clay,* but caring for the same ideals, and possessing characters and dispositions that could be matched in any European community. A hundred years had passed since an Irish pilgrim painted an unattractive picture of the habits and appearance of the Muslims, comparing them with rabbit-hunting weasels and noting their small eyes and "beards resembling those of cats".[21] Now, they had become 'handsome', 'elegant', and 'skilful horsemen'—only 'hideous' when they opposed the Christians' wishes. The educational results of a pilgrimage at this time were certainly not limited to geography.

* 'Adam's earth', in fact.

2

THE PILGRIMS

Moved by their great devotion to the Holy Places in Jerusalem, in Bethlehem, and in the Holy Land, they [Signor Roberto and his company] planned to go there to visit them, in the year 1458 . . . and they decided to set down in writing an account of their travels, beginning with the first day of their departure from the city of Milan, up to the hour of their happy return.

Roberto da Sanseverino:
Viaggio in Terra Santa, 1458[1]

The pilgrimage of the summer season in 1458—still known as the 'Spring Voyage'* although by the fifteenth century the customary date of departure had been postponed by something like six weeks—was in no way sensational. There were no tragic accidents, no kidnapping or serious extortion on the part of the Saracens, no violent quarrels among the pilgrims. For this very reason it has a particular interest; the working of the system is clearly seen and it is possible to piece together the framework of a normal tour under generally favourable conditions.

A further point of interest in this particular pilgrimage is the survival of no fewer than six narratives that cover all or part of the journey: they are compared and analysed in Appendix B. For the purposes of this study of the pilgrims'

* Formerly known as the Easter voyage; the galleys were scheduled to reach Jaffa before the end of June. At this period the 'autumn voyage' had been practically discontinued.

journey three are of outstanding interest, since they supplement and confirm—and sometimes contradict—one another in a way that sheds much light on the characters of the three authors. The longest, fullest and most factual was written by a Milanese soldier, who included, besides a vivid self-portrait, sketches of the friends who accompanied him. The second diary was written by a gentle and studious Paduan nobleman, really more at home in the lecture-room than on board ship or astride a donkey, but with a trained and receptive mind well able to appreciate the significance of all he heard and saw. The last is short and terse, packed full of interest, particularly for English readers, for it is by a West-Country Englishman whose enthusiasm was matched by his remarkable common sense. Each diarist was accompanied by several of his countrymen, so that it is possible to reconstruct—at least partially—each of the three main groups of pilgrims.

I. The Milanese

First, there was the party from Milan. The author of the *Viaggio in Terra Santa* was a notable *condottiere* named Roberto da Sanseverino, Lord of Caiazzo. This was a small hilltop town in the March of Ancona, where Roberto's family held their property. Here he was born, in 1418, but he was brought up in Milan and looked upon that city as his home. His father had died when Roberto was a small child; perhaps the fact that he was brought up by admiring women may account for his petulance and the surprise he showed when he could not always bend others to his will.

While still a boy, Roberto served his uncle,* Francesco Sforza, as a page; he was with him in 1450 when Sforza seized the Duchy of Milan and began his efficient rule. Under the guidance of this shrewd and brave general,

* Elisa, his mother, was a natural daughter of Muzio Attendolo Sforza and therefore Francesco's half-sister. Sforza accepted full responsibility for training the fatherless boy.

Roberto had every opportunity to learn the arts of chivalry and leadership and to develop military craft and skill. Francesco made use of his young kinsman in minor ways, without giving him any serious commission until he was well into his thirties, when he entrusted Roberto with the defence of Siena against one of the most famous of all the mercenary leaders of that time.* Even then, Sforza sent with Roberto his own half-brother, Corrado da Fogliano, in the hope of curbing the younger man's impetuosity. For Roberto, up to his death in 1487, when he was drowned in the River Adige, fighting an unnecessary battle against overwhelming odds, was subject to sudden fits of anger and recklessness that sometimes destroyed his judgement and led his troops to disaster.

Nevertheless, Roberto was intelligent as well as brave. He was, too, very likeable and seems to have inspired loyalty and affection in the minds of his followers. In the list of the forces employed by Sforza against the Venetian Republic,[2] Roberto is shown to have had under his command fifteen hundred cavalry and two hundred men-at-arms. Many of these were his personal friends, ambitious young soldiers anxious to serve under an established commander in order to gain experience. No doubt they hoped that they one day might succeed Roberto, but some letters[3] have survived that show a genuine desire of both men and junior officers to remain in his employment even though rewards might have been greater under some other leader.

Perhaps his peremptory and confident manner led people to accept Roberto at his own valuation; he had also very notable charm, while physically he was beautiful and splendid. These attributes stayed with him all his life. He was sixty-seven when a susceptible young woman in Verona wrote a poem[4] in praise of Roberto, who had come to that city to witness his sons' performance at a *giostra* or tournament. The young men carried off the two chief prizes, but

* Jacopo Piccinino, son of the even more famous Niccolò.

The Pilgrims

Laura Brenzoni had no eyes for them—she saw only the romantic figure of Roberto as he paraded the lists mounted on a snow-white horse. Giving rein to her enthusiasm, she rated his exploits superior to those of Hercules and Hannibal in a rapturous poem written in Latin hexameters. A Renaissance medal of Roberto shows his handsome profile; an even better portrait was painted by Sano di Pietro on one of the wooden book-covers, or *tavolette*, for the municipal archives at Siena.* Here he is represented on the occasion of his (second) marriage to a Sienese girl of noble family, clad in a rich ruby-red velvet tunic edged with fur, full sleeves to the wrist, with scarlet hose and cap.

The secretary who served him so devotedly,[5] the scholars who dedicated to him vernacular translations of learned works,[6] the harpist and trumpeter who beguiled his leisure hours,[7] the young Greek organist whom he befriended,[8] all these saw in Roberto da Sanseverino a man of wide interests, concerned with many matters outside his military career. The editor of his travel diary described Roberto as soldier rather than scribe—"uomo di spada e non di penna",[9] but his hand, although it may have been mightier with a sword, was by no means useless with a pen. At all events, in the *Viaggio* he gives a forthright account of his doings and his notions, painting his own self-portrait in colours as bright as his wedding garments in the *tavoletta* at Siena.

In the opening pages of the *Viaggio* Roberto made a note of the servants he chose to take with him on his pilgrimage. Three only were selected. One of them was charged with the planning of the journey, the hiring of horses, catering and so forth, with another to share these duties. The third was a personal servant, a German

* One of a collection in the State Archives at Siena. Here there is also a record of his wedding presents—including 'a basin and ewer of silver-gilt' given to his bride, Lucrezia Malavolti, by the *Signoria*. The marriage took place in Bologna, February 16th, 1473.

named Martin, who proved himself faithful and competent and far less susceptible to sea-sickness than the other two. Roberto listed also his companions and their attendants: details of their names and background will be found in Appendix A. on page 185. Lastly, there was the physician whose duty was to keep the whole party in good health.

This was an interesting and important person. Roberto described him as "Giovanni Martino da Parma"; for a long time he was thought to be G. M. Garbazza of that city,[10] as well known there as in Pavia, where he lectured on medical theory and practice. In one version of the *Viaggio*,[11] however, his name is given as "Giovanni Martino de Ferrariis" of Parma (also a medical doctor, also a lecturer at the university, or *Studio*, of Pavia). This is undoubtedly correct. Originally the de Ferrari family came from Pavia, where several of them practised as lawyers and physicians. Like Roberto himself Giovanni Martino had been in Milan when Sforza became Duke; he was knighted on this occasion and shown many signs of favour. He was the author of a work on poisons and their antidotes, one version of which was dedicated to Sforza[12] whom he served for a time as personal physician.* This book brought Giovanni Martino more renown than he deserved, for the greater part of it was copied from a treatise written by a Florentine physician of an earlier generation. If, as seems likely, the portrait enclosed within the large initial C at the beginning of the Florentine copy of Giovanni Martino's *Contra Venenum* depicts the author, he had a very lively countenance. His extended forefinger suggests that he is uttering the warning, against poisonous substances, contained in his prefatory letter. He has a grey beard, and glossy grey curls beneath his golden cap. The Paris manuscript has a miniature of a man writing; the pictures resemble one another closely.

* He is not to be confused with Giovanni Matteo de Ferrari of Grado who also acted as medical adviser to Francesco Sforza.

There can be little doubt that both represent the same person and that the portraits are genuine.*

Two friends that Roberto persuaded to accompany him to Palestine were fellow members of the Duke's household. They were young men from a similar background, but they differed considerably in personal qualities. Both Carlo Bosso and Giovanni Matteo Butigella belonged to families that had come originally from Pavia; they had lived in Milan for so long, however, that they considered themselves natives of that city. Bosso's father and uncle were already in the Duke's service when the young Carlo was allotted to the Duchess as a page. He acted jointly with his father[13] as castellan of one of the Milanese fortresses; otherwise he does not figure in the records. Although his brother addressed a poem to him[14] the year after his return from Palestine, Carlo himself is not known to have shown talent or inclination for literature. He seems, nevertheless, to have been a pleasant young man, skilled in all chivalrous practices. He lost interest in the extended pilgrimage Roberto had planned and, for some personal reason, returned home early. Butigella, on the other hand, was loyal and unselfish, with strong family feeling and affection for his companions. He was the youngest of Tomasino Butigella's three sons; he himself had two boys by his wife Bianca Visconti.† It seems to have been a particularly united family— Giovanni Matteo laboriously writing a book for his eldest brother, and the middle one, Conradino, going to much trouble in attempting to meet Giovanni Matteo when he returned from his travels.

* Dr. Elisabeth Pellegrin is of the opinion that both MSS. were written in Milan and that they probably emanated from the workshop of the 'Maître des Vitae Imperateur'. I am greatly indebted to her for her help in this, as in many other matters.

† She was descended from Uberto, brother of Matteo I Visconti, Lord of Milan. She died in 1486. When she married Butigella, Bianca was the widow of Ettore Furloni. Their elder boy, Filippo Maria, in due course became a Ducal Councillor.

Like many of his kind, Butigella was interested in books and scholarly studies: he had several humanist friends who accepted him as one of themselves. Among them were the Decembrio brothers, Angelo and the more famous Pier Candido, with whom he corresponded.[15] Angelo described Butigella as "interested in the humane arts" and praised him as "studiosus". The books in his collection were well chosen and beautifully produced; his library is evidence of his discriminating taste.[16] What set Butigella apart from his companions was the fact that he alone had first-hand knowledge of the Near East. Six years earlier Duke Francesco had sent him with two colleagues on a mission to Alexandria. One of his fellows was the same Corrado da Fogliano who was associated with Sanseverino in the defence of Siena, the other a trusted official of the household.* Sforza sent two letters to his emissaries during the late summer of 1452;[17] it seems that they stayed in Alexandria for several weeks or months to carry out the instructions that he gave them. Since Butigella was an intelligent and observant person, the experience that he gained at this time proved very useful when he and Sanseverino were planning their return journey at the end of the tour.

Since leave of absence had been freely granted by the Duke of Milan, there was no reason for the Archbishop to refuse the travellers their licence. Messengers were sent out to arrange sleeping-quarters on the journey to Venice, and elaborate schemes had to be set on foot for the stabling of horses and hiring of boats. Ambassadors and consuls were notified of their coming; everything possible was done to ensure that at any rate the first stage of the pilgrimage would be smooth and comfortable——whatever might happen later on. All that remained to be done before starting was for the pilgrims to sew red crosses upon the 'grey'† gowns and

---

* Pietro Pusterlo; there are a number of his letters in the State Archives at Milan.

† Really, brown, cf. the Franciscans' robes.

hats that they would wear as a sign of humility and to arrange their gear. Personal possessions were sewn into canvas bags and carefully corded, for there was no knowing how wet and dirty the baggage might become on its way to the quayside in Venice, nor what would happen to it on board the galley.

By the end of April, 1458, the Milanese party was ready to set out. April 30th was a Sunday; the prospective pilgrims went with their families and friends to hear Mass before starting on their travels. Leave-taking was, as might be expected, a protracted business. It was conducted, moreover, "with much sobbing and with many sighs", so that it was two o'clock in the afternoon before Butigella and Bosso had nerved themselves to don the brown robes that proclaimed their pious intention. They had dined in their own homes in order to enjoy the company of their families up to the last possible moment, before setting out to join Sanseverino at his town house in the centre of Milan. On arrival, they found a large number of friends gathered to bid the party goodbye; further caresses and embracings had then to be sustained.

According to Roberto's calculation,[18] at least two thousand people saw them off on the first stage of their journey, following them on foot or on horseback several miles beyond the city limits. These well-wishers dropped off in twos and threes, returning to their homes while the pilgrims pressed on towards Pavia. About half-way between Milan and that city they paused to water their horses and to take some refreshment themselves; it was late in the evening before they had covered the further ten miles to Pavia. As Butigella had many friends and kindred here, the party received the warmest possible welcome from all the citizens. Indeed, two young nobles were so carried away by their enthusiasm that they insisted upon joining the pilgrimage and made hasty preparations to do so. These were Domenico da Calcenoni from Lodi, and a friend of

Carlo Bosso named Fenone degli Eustachio whose home
was in Pavia. Students and masters from the famous
university crowded round the travellers; they were offered
such abundant hospitality that they were not able to get
to bed till nearly dawn.

The chief point in visiting Pavia, apart from Butigella's
natural wish to bid his friends goodbye, was to board a ship
there that would take the party down the Ticino river to its
junction with the Po, and thence nearly all the way to
Venice. This was much the most pleasant and convenient
way to travel across northern Italy, although it would have
been quicker to go by road; on their return from Venice the
following January—although it was then mid-winter—
Roberto and his companions completed the overland
journey in less than five days, whereas the outward trip
lasted for nearly eight. On Monday morning, May 1st,
they all attended Mass in order to receive the special pilgrims' blessing before making their way—still accompanied
by most of the inhabitants of Pavia—to the river bank. The
boat lay ready with their baggage stowed neatly under
cover; grooms waited to lead the horses back to their stables
in Milan. The pilgrims stepped aboard, taking their leave
"with great tenderness and effusion of tears". By eleven
o'clock they were on their way to Piacenza.

For the first few hours the travellers occupied themselves
with their devotions, repeating together litanies and the
seven penitential psalms. As dinnertime drew near, however,
practical considerations had to be met. The first thing to do
was to choose a seneschal or man of affairs to be responsible
for all arrangements. Since Giovanni da Glusiano, of Carlo
Bosso's household, was said to be "adept at such matters"
he was given the appointment, which he seems to have
fulfilled with credit. The forty miles from Pavia were
covered in eleven hours "in great amity and with the utmost
goodwill". It was nearly dark when they came to Piacenza,
but it was still possible to discern the crowd of citizens

gathered on the river bank to welcome them. Arrangements had been made for them to stay in the house of the Chamberlain, Messer Jacopo Pormano, who held an appointment in the Duke's household and was therefore well known to all the Milanese pilgrims. Messer Jacopo had prepared for them "a supper so well arranged and furnished that it lacked nothing even a king could have demanded". It certainly satisfied the travellers, who did the hospitality full justice. Immediately after this grand meal they went to bed and slept till well on into the next morning, which dawned grey and cold.

So far everything had gone marvellously well for the pilgrims. Now it was the weather that failed them, for the rain streamed down relentlessly and a chilly head-wind blew against them all the way to Chioggia (or 'Gioza', in Roberto's provincial spelling). Before ever they reached Cremona everyone was soaked to the skin. As he sat helplessly in his sodden clothes Roberto was exasperated by their slow progress, for the gusts of wind kept turning the boat off her course and driving her against the reedy banks. The actual danger was probably less than he believed at the time, but it was a relief to them all when the towers of Cremona came into view. Wearily the passengers landed, stripped off their wet clothes, supped, and at last lay down to rest.

Day followed day, all wet and cold and depressing. The party met generous hospitality, the Marquis of Mantua sent them presents, Borso d'Este Duke of Modena had ordered his factor to supply them with all they needed, but their spirits remained low until at last, on Saturday, May 6th, the weather cleared. Now they could make good progress; that night they moored their boat in the harbour at Chioggia, in preparation for the last stage of their journey to Venice. On Sunday the 7th the pilgrims attended an early Mass, worshipping at the altar of Our Lady and gaining thereby many indulgences. The sun was shining by the time they were ready to leave. The wind now favoured them, since they were travelling northward, so that they were able to cross the lagoon in good time and without mishap.

As the buildings of Venice rose to meet them, first shrouded in haze, then shining in the sunlight, the pilgrims' excitement grew. So far, the expedition had been no more than a journey between two Italian towns that might have been undertaken for any secular purpose; now, the real adventure had begun. Each pilgrim felt exaltation or trepidation, according to his temperament, as they approached their moorings and prepared to land. Word had arrived of their coming: Roberto's influential connections opened to him many doors that would have remained immovable in the face of ordinary pilgrims. The Marquis of Varese, Milanese ambassador to the Republic, had arranged to accommodate the whole party in his palace. Roberto acknowledged the hospitality in the first gracious words he had uttered since the bad weather interfered with his plans, leaving him grumbling and sodden with rain that he seemed to think was aimed at him personally. "They were received," he wrote, "with as much honour and affectionate greeting as it is possible to imagine; in the house of the Marquis everything was provided for the needs of the whole company in the best possible way." He added that the palace was "convenient and very comfortable".[19] The galley was not yet due to sail, there would be time for sightseeing and for visiting friends and kinsmen as well as for shopping and for completing arrangements for the voyage. These nine days before their departure were some of the most pleasant of the whole trip, with everything to look forward to and all illusions as yet intact.

II. The Paduans

In Padua at this time there were some more pilgrims who intended to make the Spring Voyage. They were too well acquainted with local weather conditions to move to Venice before they were convinced that the galley really was about to sail. Their passages had been booked some time earlier—as soon, indeed, as it became known who would be the captain in charge of the expedition. Padua was less than a day's ride from Venice, so there was no difficulty about passing messages to and fro.

The two pilgrims whose names are known—it seems likely that they were accompanied by friends and certainly by several servants—were cousins bound by a strong tie of affection and common interests. They were members of the illustrious Paduan family of Capodilista that had had honourable connections with the government of that city and its famous university through several generations. The younger of the two was Antonio; there is a striking portrait of him in a manuscript that records the distinctions of his family.[20] It would seem that Antonio was about thirty years old at the time of his pilgrimage, already a wealthy and successful man with a villa and gardens just outside Padua that were famous for their beauty and extent.[21] The elder Capodilista cousin, Gabriele, also had a charming villa with pleasure-grounds where he held parties for his studious and artistic friends; it lay on the road to Abano about three miles beyond the suburbs of Padua. It was here that he held a reunion in January 1459 for several of the pilgrims after their return from Palestine.

Gabriele was the eldest son of a very distinguished father, who had taught continuously in the *Studio* for more than forty years, except when he was away acting as ambassador for his city at the Council of Basel and on other important missions. Gabriele was either less able or less ambitious: he seems to have studied at Paris and Bologna[22] without achieving any special distinction; diplomatic triumphs he left to his brother Francesco, who was also a lawyer and a renowned poet. Gabriele had a very strongly provincial love of his city and the surrounding countryside.

That Padua was constantly in his mind when he was writing the *Itinerario in Terra Santa* is shown by at least four direct references and also by oblique allusions when he was describing the scenery of Palestine. The River Jordan reminded him of the "turbid waters" of the Paduan Bacchi-glione,[23] and a great cistern was "as large as the baths at Abano"[24] close to his own home. When he reached Bethle-hem, Gabriele had only to see the grotto under the high altar to recall the Cathedral at Padua and the architecture of Santa Giustina.[25] Between the churches of the Holy Sepulchre and his beloved S. Antonio, Gabriele drew a close comparison.[26] Gabriele was a very civilized person, kind and gentle; he had great personal integrity and was com-pletely devoid of arrogance. His *Itinerario* reflects his character; there are no personal diatribes against officials or fellow-pilgrims, he makes little of his personal sufferings but has great compassion for those of others, his record of day-to-day happenings is careful and accurate without being either dull or lifeless. This is, indeed, a very delightful book, less amusing than Roberto's *Viaggio*, less trenchant than William Wey's advice to pilgrims, but sincere and sensitive and never pompous.

When at last the day came for their departure, we learn from the *Itinerario* that the cousins, with all their relations and friends, went to hear Mass in the basilica of S. Antonio. Afterwards they all took a meal together. This was Tuesday, May 16th; at about mid-day the Capodilista cousins em-barked with their servants in a boat lying ready for them alongside the bank of the River Brenta. Their craft glided over the still, opaque waters, past the noble villas of Venetian magnates, past gardens where fountains played, steadily on towards the lagoon. By eight o'clock they were in Venice. At once they began to buy "the small things still needed to complete their pilgrims' outfit". Next day, "finding the weather good, they gave thanks to Our Lady and to their special patrons St. Luke, S. Prosdocimo, and

Santa Giustina". Then they made their way out to the galley, where they found their travelling companions already aboard. All that was needed now was a fair and a favourable wind.

III. The Englishmen

Long before the Milanese set out for Pavia and the River Po numbers of northern (or 'ultramontane') pilgrims had been making their way laboriously towards Venice. The uncertainties of the journey were so great, the hazards so many, that pilgrims from remote countries were likely to allow too large a time-margin: this could—and often did—lead to financial embarrassment in Venice when pilgrims neared the end of their resources before the pilgrimage proper had even started. Few were as bold as the Englishman who, in this year 1458, cut his journey so fine that he arrived in Venice when the galley was "on the point of departure" so that all he had to do, said one of his biographers,[27] was to "step on board" before she sailed. This was the English 'milord', John Tiptoft, Earl of Worcester. He is a good example of those who found it convenient to absent themselves from home, for a time, under cover of making a pilgrimage, for matters were becoming very difficult for him in England, torn as he was between rival factions. There were, however, further considerations that led John Tiptoft to Venice at this time. From his Oxford days—he was a member of University College, not Balliol as is sometimes wrongly stated—Tiptoft had planned to make the Jerusalem pilgrimage. Indeed, he discussed the matter with a fellow undergraduate[28] who advised him to take with him an artist to draw pictures of the birds and beasts and other strange sights that he would see in the Holy Land. If he did so, the pictures do not seem to have survived, although other patrons of his generation were more fortunate: the

Pilgrim Book of Gabriel Muffel* springs readily to mind.

John Tiptoft's father died while he was at Oxford; he had to go back to his home in Cambridgeshire to take up his inheritance. Thereafter he was busy looking after the family estates in England and Wales, until he was swept into politics and found himself appointed Lord Treasurer at the early age of twenty-four. Tiptoft served King Henry VI in various capacities, being rewarded for his services by the grant of the Earldom of Worcester and other royal favours,[29] but his personal loyalty was to his own cousin Edward Duke of York, later King Edward IV. As long as Henry VI had no heir the matter was fairly simple, but when a son was born to Henry and Margaret of Anjou the whole position was changed overnight. The Milanese ambassador maliciously reported that the child must be the son of the Holy Spirit,[30] but the young Prince Edward was indubitably heir to the throne and York's expectation of the succession was shattered. Tiptoft was allied not only with the Duke of York but also (by marriage and by friendship) with his strongest supporters, the Nevilles. He was not the man to balance himself between the parties without committing himself to either; Tiptoft had neither the skill nor the taste for such gymnastics. His decision to make his pilgrimage at a time when civil war seemed imminent has sometimes been called cowardly or irresponsible, but a more charitable judgement was put forward by Tiptoft's seventeenth-century biographer Thomas Fuller. With his usual felicity Fuller wrote: ". . . this Earl could not be discourteous to Henry VI who had so much advanced him, nor disloyall to Edward IV in whom the right of the Crown lay. Consulting his own safety, he resolved on this expedient, for a time to quit his own and to visit the Holy Land."[31] Moreover, a young man who later became his secretary

* Written just ten years later. The manuscript with text and pictures can be seen in the British Museum (MS. Egerton 1900). Reproductions from it are in this book.

openly commended him for preferring peace to war.[32]

As a person John Tiptoft was notable for his freedom from pomp and self-importance; many of his friends and correspondents were humble people who could not possibly help him in the career that had been forced upon him, but who shared his bookish and artistic interests. He was loyal and faithful to his old friends and sincerely religious. Up to this time Tiptoft had shown nothing of the ruthless cruelty that marred his later life and brought him the nickname of The Butcher.* His travelling companions certainly found him pleasant and courteous, and were very glad to accept the ministrations of his chaplains.

Both as Lord Treasurer and as 'Keeper of the Sea' Tiptoft had been brought into contact with the commanders of the Venetian galleys trading with London, who brought presents of "syruped confections of green ginger melon and quince" in majolica jars or in exquisite glass flasks from Murano: these were intended to placate the Treasurer and win his favour. Since Tiptoft is known to have corresponded with one of these captains[33] it is possible that he and his party came directly to Venice by sea in one of the returning merchantmen, together with a cargo of Cotswold wool and hides. Certainly he and his retinue of twenty-seven —"mostly priests"—travelled independently of the main body of pilgrims who came across the Alps, following the itinerary so carefully worked out by generations of travellers.

It was also in this year, 1458, that William Wey composed the main part of his guide-book,† recording in it his own experiences and thoughtfully giving an alternative route for travellers who might have to deflect their course

---

* It must in fairness be pointed out that this name was bestowed upon him (after his death) by Tudor chroniclers who were masters of propaganda —the same writers who claimed that Richard III was born with a full set of teeth and endowed him with a mythical hump back as well as every vice known to mankind.

† He made another journey to Palestine in 1462, but this added little to his experiences.

in the event of some natural or political obstruction. His own itinerary is traced from Dover to Venice; at different points along its course a trickle of pilgrims from distant parts of Europe, or from the provinces through which the road passed, joined the main body. Wey did not find it necessary to describe in detail the inns and hospices on the route, for these were well known to travellers, whether merchants or pilgrims. All the Alpine passes, and especially the Brenner—open as it was for almost all the year—were well supplied with houses or chalets where pilgrims could find not only food and lodging, but also stabling for their horses, with facilities for washing their linen and for curing minor ailments. The native *marones* of the Great St. Bernard had been established there ever since the twelfth century; they were ready to help the pilgrims over difficult sections of the road and there were similar guides on some of the other passes. Their activities were valuable to travellers who felt a very natural timidity and were liable to be daunted by the unknown, though not all were as timorous as Adam of Usk who insisted upon being blindfolded because he could not bear to see the horrors of the St. Gotthard, preferring to be transported on a sled as part of the pilgrims' baggage.

William Wey himself was certainly not timorous; he was cheerful and practical and, despite his fifty-one years, as eager as any younger man to see and do everything within his power. Little is known of his background, beyond the fact that he came from the West Country, but his sturdy character is clearly revealed in his own book. That he was a Fellow of Exeter College, Oxford, and an original Fellow of the new foundation at Eton, is well established. It is clear, too, from his *Itineraries* that he made two pilgrimages to Palestine and one to Compostella. If these slender facts were all the evidence for his existence he would be a shadowy figure indeed. In the *Itineraries*, however, he comes vividly to life. Here he shows himself as a realist, characterized

by directness and good sense. His invincible good humour
shines through the pages of his book. Wey's advice though
shrewd is never waspish; he patiently considers the needs
of those less intelligent and resourceful than himself.
Sometimes his own experiences colour the instructions that
he gives. For instance, when writing about the necessity
for procuring a licence, he points out that this may take
time and perseverance and will probably cost a considerable
sum of money. He himself had had to approach not only
the bishop of his diocese but also King Henry VI in person.
This was because Wey was a member of a royal foundation
(Eton College). His annual six weeks' leave could not
possibly be stretched to cover the period of his pilgrimage:
although King Henry wrote to the Fellows[34] nine months
before Wey planned to set out, that the licence had been
granted to him—"having tendre consideration unto his
blessed purpos and entent"—there were still many payments
and formalities to be negotiated.

When all their material needs had been supplied, the
pilgrims still had to conjure up a placid and good-tempered
approach to the problems and crises that must occur from
time to time even in a well-ordered expedition. Wey's
bidding to them to be "of good chere" was not the least
important of his exhortations.

3

VENICE

Venice is a large and handsome town, ancient and
commercial, and built in the middle of the sea.
Bertrand de la Brocquière, in 1432[1]

I

The house where the Milanese were staying stood in a
fashionable quarter of Venice. Lesser pilgrims had to be
content with lodgings or inns of their own finding, often
at some distance from the city centre. Few made arrangements in advance, for advice given by returned travellers
was sometimes unreliable and often out of date. A list of
addresses was part of the pilgrim lore handed on from
generation to generation; certainly this advance information
did something to smooth the path to Jerusalem, but it was
embarrassing for travellers to arrive late at night, unsure
of their whereabouts, only to discover that the innkeeper
they sought had died or sold his business. It was, of course,
natural for pilgrims to make for lodgings where their
countrymen had stayed. Here they would expect to find
someone who understood their language and could cater
for their special needs. In this way inns became associated
with particular nationalities. Germans, for instance, went
in large numbers to the great inn of St. George,* close to
the *Fondaco dei Tedeschi*, or trading centre, where Germans
stored their goods in a giant warehouse. A large restaurant
stood nearby, where these nationals could buy beer and
sausages.[2]

* More commonly called The Flute.

47

An inn that was very cosmopolitan in character, where traders and pilgrims of many different races used to assemble in order to exchange their news and views, was *La Storione* on the Rialto.[3] Here, tongues and dialects from all over Europe could be heard voicing opinions of every shade; it says much for the conduct of the inn that the visitors seem to have lived in perfect amity. The more timid travellers, however, continued to frequent lodgings recommended by their countrymen, partly through fear of the unknown, partly because they imagined that they could live there more frugally.

Every inn-keeper was bound to keep a register of those staying on his premises. The names of the guests had to be given in to the appropriate office within three days of the visitor's arrival: failure to conform to this regulation meant not only a fine, but also a black mark against the hotelier's name that might well prove indelible.

It should not be assumed that Venetian inn-keepers and shop-owners were necessarily rapacious, nor that they failed to care for their guests and give them good value for their money. There was a special committee of the Senate, named the *Cattaveri*, who existed to keep a watch over the visitors' interests. It was their business to grant licences, to examine premises and to control prices. They scrutinized the inn-keepers as carefully and as closely as they examined captains of the galleys who would take the pilgrims on the next stage. The *Cattaveri* were also ready to hear any complaints made by the visitors concerning discomfort or extortion. Nor did they stop at this; to ensure protection of unsophisticated pilgrims they appointed a dozen 'piazza guides'. These were all good linguists; they were prepared to help their clients to make purchases, to show them the way to their lodgings when they were lost, above all to explain to them the intricacies of foreign currency.

These guides were known as *tholomarii*; their duties were taken very seriously by the Venetian Senate for, had they been corrupt, the *tholomarii* could have done great damage to Venice's reputation for fair dealing. They were made to take an oath binding them to observe the rules laid down for their conduct. These were detailed and intricate, but one guiding principle ran through them all: the *tholomarii* existed for the benefit of the pilgrims, they were not expected to line their own pockets. In particular, they were forbidden to accept commissions from the tradesmen whose shops they visited. Because the guides were paid a decent salary, tips from clients were considered unnecessary; indeed, from time to time their acceptance was forbidden. In actual fact it was not possible to prevent rich pilgrims from trying to buy preferential treatment, but the practice was certainly frowned upon. The number of *tholomarii* had been raised from eight to twelve by the mid-fifteenth century; they served in shifts, two always being on duty from dawn till dusk, while a rota was formed to deal with any emergency during the night. Although they were allowed (singly) to take an hour off for their mid-day meal, any attempt to institute a 'tea-break' (or its equivalent) was immediately disallowed. From the pilgrims' point of view the system of 'piazza guides' was highly satisfactory, for it saved them from all worry as well as from exploitation. It was the pride of the Venetian Senate to give such good service: it was also excellent business.

Then, as now, tempting shops fringed the Piazza S. Marco. Here pilgrims could buy everything that was necessary for the voyage as well as much that was not. Most people needed bedding—a mattress, feather-bed, pillow, two pairs of sheets and a quilt could all be bought for the standard price of three ducats; if they were returned in good condition at the end of the voyage half the purchase price would be refunded. The shrewd author of *Information for Pilgrims unto the Holy Land* advised purchasers to "marke his hous and his name that ye bought it of". To buy these necessities seemed fair enough; there were few who cared

to go to the expense and trouble of bringing bed linen
from home. Changes of clothing, spare shirts, strong perfumes, insecticides, guide-books in several languages, and
manuals of good behaviour could all be bought in this region,
also rosaries, relics, and souvenirs of every description.

Every day boats from Chioggia and the neighbouring
islands brought vegetables and fruit to the quayside. At this
time of year they carried peas, beans, and cherries. Some had
nosegays of flowers and herbs; all were piled high with the
brightly coloured produce. Ranged in booths and on stalls
were quantities of good things to catch the pilgrim's eye
and whet his appetite. The local cream cheeses must be
eaten quickly before they could turn rancid, but there were
various kinds of harder cheese from Lombardy that would
make palatable the ship's biscuit that the pilgrims must
expect on board the galley once they were well out to sea.
Best of all was the fresh, pale gorgonzola, deepening in
strength and hue as the voyage proceeded, that brought to
the Milanese pleasant memories of home. There were
sausages, too, from Bologna and elsewhere, as well as every
kind of sweetmeat from comfits to the syrup of ginger
commended by William Wey as a means of comforting
the stomach.

In the bakers' shops could be seen every imaginable
kind of bread and biscuit; one pilgrim found these of such
incredible beauty that "the sight . . . tempts even a man who
is surfeited to eat again".[4] On the other hand, meat from
the market by the Rialto (where prices were sometimes lower
than in the Piazza) was said to be of poor quality and to
have far too much bone with it. Poultry was dear and apt
to be tough; the local fish was scarce and bad. Experienced
pilgrims shunned these foods, concentrating upon wine,
cheese, sweetmeats and spices. Some preferred not to rely
upon the eggs and poultry that might be offered them when
the ship reached port but took with them a hen-coop full
of fowls—"a cage for half a dozen of hennes or chekys

to have wyth you in the . . . galey for ye shall haue nede to
them many tyme. And bye you half a bushell of myle[t]
sede . . . for theym." The author of the *Information* thought
of everything. He gave further advice to his pilgrims on the
choice of "Confections, Confortatives, Laxatives, Restric-
tives", specifying green ginger, almonds, rice, figs and
raisins for these purposes. Saffron, cloves and mace were
recommended to give interest to tasteless dishes or to cover
flavours that might be abhorrent. The practical William
Wey went one step further, adding some excellent advice
about cooking utensils. "Also take with yew", he says, "a
lytyl cawdren and frying pan, dysches, platterys, sawserrys
of tre [wood], cuppes of glas, a grater for brede, and such
necessaryes."

When their shopping was done and the pilgrims had
gathered together their gear, the cypress chests with strong
locks, the hen-coops, the bedding, the barrels of water and
wine, and all their other provisions, they were free to indulge
in sightseeing. Not only the true 'foreigners', the ultramontanes, but also the Italians were astounded by the richness and variety of the Venetian buildings and commodities.
Indeed, the best of all descriptions of Venice in the mid-
fifteenth century was written by a Sienese.[5] "A very lovely
city," is his verdict, "the buildings of which are separated
only by canals along which flows the sea water, in place of
streets. The large canals are wide enough to admit a battle-
ship with its oars. There are also roads paved with brick
where one can walk on foot. Hither comes merchandise
from almost all over the world, nor is there in Europe a
nobler emporium. Merchants from all the west bring their
goods here, and collect the wares of the orient. They have
also a well-equipped naval armament-store which they call
the Arsenal, fitted with every kind of machine, where they
build warships and all kinds of other craft without inter-
mission. . . . The city is all of brick . . . but if their power
continues it will soon be all of marble. Already the houses

of the nobles are encrusted all over with marble and glitter with much gold. A very fine church of oriental marble has been built in the middle of the city to St. Mark the Evangelist, and the arches of this church are all gilded over with the craft they call mosaic. Here, they say . . . is a treasure which exceeds the wealth of kings, adorned with rubies, diamonds, emeralds . . . once the well-filled treasury of the Emperors of the East. . . . They say that the pinnacle of the Campanile is gilded with 60,000 ducats worth of gold. . . . There are also throughout the city many other churches and monasteries admirable for their magnificence and workmanship. Daily that city grows, for there are no walls around it, only water."

All tourists went to see the Arsenal, where the great galleys or battleships were fitted out with gear and armaments. One observer[6] saw ten of them in line being towed slowly past the windows of the storehouses—as though they were on a conveyor belt. By the time they reached the end of the dock each galley had its full complement of stores and equipment. The pilgrim ships were built in yards nearby; they also were well found, though not standardized to such a high degree. Tourists often visited the glass-works at Murano, standing amazed at the precision of the craftsmen and the brittle delicacy of the treasures they produced, but the strongest impression that they carried home with them was of Venice herself, lavish, bejewelled, and singular. Bruges had her waterways, London her Goldsmiths' Row, many cities had ancient and wonderful churches and palaces, but Venice had everything. While the visitors admired they also envied; even though Venetian magnates in their pride and confidence might dress themselves in plain black gowns, nothing could hide the splendour of their position as merchant princes with a long and successful family history behind them. Those who wanted to taunt the Venetians might call them fishes or speak in exasperation of "that fisherman's boorishness which they had inherited from their forefathers",[7] but it was impossible for anyone to disregard their supreme efficiency or to deny its success made manifest in this city of pearl and gold.

II

Immediately after Mass on the first morning of their arrival, Roberto and his friends went to call upon the Doge; their shopping, when "every man gathered to himself all those things that he might need upon the journey", was put off to another day. A new Doge had recently been installed;* he showed himself approachable and hospitable, welcoming his visitors most warmly. His conversation was amiable; he seemed well informed about the pilgrims' plans. He made them, too, small gifts in token of his interest in their doings. This personal welcome extended to the more important visitors to his city was part of the Doge's normal duties; but Maripietro seems to have had the art of making his callers feel that they had been selected personally to receive his favours. This Doge never became intoxicated by power or remote from ordinary citizens; he ruled competently and constitutionally without attempting to shape the destiny of the Republic. He was, in fact, something of a time-server; as far as the pilgrims were concerned, however, he could not have shown himself more helpful.

The pilgrim traffic was, of course, one of Venice's most lucrative sources of income. The tolls that had to be paid, the customs dues, and the charges that the captains made for carrying the pilgrims in their galleys amounted to a very considerable revenue. Out of the fifty ducats paid by each traveller as the standard fare, rather more than a third reached the treasury of the Venetian Senate in one way or another. Some paid a little more in order to gain extra favours and comforts, others who could not pay the full rate were taken more cheaply; fellow pilgrims, the captain

* Pasquale Maripietro.

himself, or occasionally the Senate might allow a supplement
to make up the difference. The more pilgrims there were,
the better the Venetian Senate was pleased; more money
came into the exchequer through tolls, more money was
spent in the shops, the tradesmen could pay higher taxes
—in every way the government prospered, an economic fact
very well known to the Doge and his advisers. No wonder
he could afford to invite the richer travellers to dinner and
to give donations to the most poverty stricken of the Irish
pilgrims.

Well satisfied with their reception at the Doge's Palace,
the Milanese went off to inspect the two galleys appointed
for the Spring Voyage that year. They found the booking
offices in the Piazza S. Marco, where each captain had set
up his banner of white silk embellished with a red cross,
mounted on a tall spear, outside the west door of the
Cathedral. It was usual to pay the fare and sign the contract
a few days before sailing, so that payment and conditions
could be registered and checked in the official records. A
highly experienced captain—or *patrono*—named Antonio
Loredan had been successful that year in the auction that
determined to whom should be given licence to sail; it
was in his galley, the *Loredana*, that the Milanese booked
their passages, after a careful inspection of its amenities.

Much was bound to depend upon the captain's ability
and temperament. It was in his power to make the lot of his
passengers either tolerable or wretched. If he were arrogant
and unapproachable, the pilgrims would not dare to ask
his help or advice in small matters; they in turn would
become awkward and sullen. A tactful *patrono* could smooth
out difficulties without appearing to do so; a wise one would
see to it that his officers and crew treated every passenger
with courtesy. The galleys were built, owned, and officered
by members of patrician local families. Sometimes a son
might act as *patrono* of his father's ship; more often the
master sailed in his own galley that had been built in the

Venetian shipyards to his own design. In Antonio Loredan, descendant of many generations of notable seamen, the pilgrims were fortunate to find a *patrono* of strong character whose technical skill was matched by his long experience of pilgrims and Saracens and their relations with one another. There could have been no better choice of interpreter and guide.

The pilgrims were fortunate, too, in their ship, for the *Loredana* was newly commissioned and fresh from her trials. Among the officers was young Niccolò Loredan, Antonio's eldest son. He accompanied his father to gain experience for the day when he too would sail as master in a pilgrim galley. No special responsibility was given to him until the *Loredana* reached Jaffa, when his father deputed to him some delicate negotiations with the Franciscan brothers of Mount Syon. The crew included carpenters and 'calkers' to keep the ship in repair; the sailors were veterans of many pilgrim voyages. Then there were the rowers, or *galeotti*, on whose strength and tenacity everyone's safety was likely to depend. The popular image of these *galeotti* as 'galley slaves' is entirely false; a century later condemned criminals, or prisoners of war, were commonly chained to benches and forced to pull the oars in the great galleys or battleships, but throughout the fifteenth century the rowers were free men of Venice and her dependent lands. Recruiting stations were set up for them in the Piazza; men between the ages of twenty-five and forty could sign on for a period of years or in some instances for a single voyage. They were paid for their services and were allowed to go ashore to trade—often they found it highly profitable to sell goods to the passengers, as well as to natives in the ports where they touched. The *galeotti* were always glad to lay down their oars and snatch up weapons—cross-bows, arrows and lances—should the galley be attacked by pirates. They were generally tough and rugged in character and sometimes insubordinate. On the return journey from Acre to Ancona, in Francesco di

Alberto's ship,* the *galeotti* were always arguing with the *patrono*, or offering him unsought advice, or over-staying their shore leave, not at all in the manner of slaves; Roberto da Sanseverino represents them as singularly independent in outlook and character.

Their business settled, the friends chartered a boat and went in it across the lagoon to meet Alessandro Sforza, brother to the Duke of Milan—and a noted general—who had just returned "from foreign parts".[8] Since word had been brought them of Alessandro's coming, they were able to time his arrival with some exactness. They welcomed him "with a thousand kisses", cheerfully escorting him to the lodging allotted to him by the Senate on the island of S. Giorgio. Next morning, at an early hour, Roberto and his companions were back at S. Giorgio; after some talk with Alessandro Sforza they went sightseeing together, then, as it was the Eve of the Ascension, everyone attended Vespers in the church of S. Marco.

The Feast of the Ascension dawned bright and clear. Roberto crossed to the Island in order to escort his uncle Alessandro to the Doge's Palace, for they had been invited to join in the famous Ascension Day ceremony of the Wedding of the Sea and to accompany the Doge personally in his traditional barge, the *Bucentaur*. Sanseverino describes the ceremony "in case there are any who have not seen it"; although many others have written about the pageant[9] his report has a sharp and eye-witness quality that lends it a special value. The procession, he says, was headed by the Cross, carried by the clergy. The six guilds of S. Marco followed close behind, bearing their silken banners, followed by the members of the *Signoria* marching to the sound of silver trumpets. The Doge himself rode high upon a gilded throne, above his head a *baldacchino*, or canopy, of gold brocade lined with blue silk bespangled with gold stars. On his head the Doge wore his *biretta* of office;

* See Chapter 15.

behind him guards carried a splendid sword of silver gilt. Behind the *Signoria* came all the merchants and gentlemen of Venice, proud families with famous names, mustered according to their rank and age.

Since they were distinguished visitors, Roberto and Sforza enjoyed prominent places in the procession and on board the *Bucentaur*. Indeed, at the climax of the ceremony they were invited to stand on either side of the Doge himself. The beauty and richness of this vessel delighted them, adorned as it was with silken draperies, its frame carved and painted and gilded into the semblance of a tabernacle. Golden bells hung from the canopy that bore the Maripietro coat of arms together with the shields of former famous Doges. The barge was propelled by three hundred newly-painted oars that flashed and sparkled in the sunlight. As the flotilla passed out to sea, in preparation for the great moment when the Patriarch would pronounce his blessing, it was joined by innumerable small boats. Keeping as near to the *Bucentaur* as they dared, a party of keen-eyed divers stood poised to plunge after the golden ring that the Doge would fling into the sea as an emblem of the Espousal. To recover this ring was not only thrifty; it was also a token of good luck: to snatch it before it reached the bottom was a feat of the utmost skill.

When all was accomplished, the whole company turned about, setting course for the church of S. Niccolò on the Lido, in order to offer there thanksgiving and devotions. The Patriarch of Venice displayed the church's holy relics to Roberto and Alessandro, who viewed them with reverence and paid the customary gratuity. Afterwards everyone re-embarked in the same order as before. Swiftly they returned to the Doge's Palace, where the two Milanese, together with the ambassadors and other important guests, expected to dine with the Doge. Roberto decided, however, that he must decline this invitation since he still had much to do before the galley sailed.

On Friday, May 12th, word came to the pilgrims that they must come aboard the galleys the following Sunday. Feverish last-minute packing and preparations of many kinds kept them busy all that day and the next. Early on Sunday morning the Milanese and other pilgrims rowed the two miles out from Venice to the galley's moorings. Most of them elected to sleep aboard that night, but Roberto and his friends returned to their comfortable lodgings for what they expected to be their last night ashore for many weeks.

In the meantime, the English 'milord', John Tiptoft, had arrived; the same Sunday he negotiated with the Senate an arrangement that did much to promote the comfort and well-being of the whole party. He decided that not only would he sail in the *Loredana*, he would also engage her *patrono* as his personal courier and guide. It was not difficult to gain permission from the *Cattaveri* to retain Loredan's services. There were precedents for this; it was not the first time that the Senate had granted important foreigners such a favour, indeed, it was thought to be a good advertisement of Venetian services and capabilities. The contract was drawn up with all speed; it is still to be seen in the Venetian State Archives,[10] among the Deliberations of the *Cattaveri*. "There has come to our city", say these officials, ". . . a certain English Lord, of high importance and reputation in his own land, who wishes to visit the Holy Sepulchre. And he purposes to sail in the galley *Loredana* . . . and wishes to have the company, in visiting the Holy Places, of the noble Antonio Lauredan." In order to free the *patrono* for his new duties, his second-in-command was appointed captain of the galley and given responsibility for navigating and sailing her to Jaffa. This was Loredan's cousin, Baldessare Diedo, who had been a shipmate on previous voyages. He, too, was a good and tried seaman, although he had less experience of negotiating business with the Saracens, a matter in which Loredan excelled.

An Unfavourable Wind

During the night of May 14th-15th the wind shifted
to an unfavourable quarter, so that next morning the
Milanese, when they had boarded the small boat that was
to take them out to the galley, found it impossible to make
any headway. The rowers pulled on their oars with all their
might but made no progress at all. Exasperated by this ill
fortune, Roberto and his friends had to return once again
to their lodging. It was not until mid-afternoon on Wednesday, May 17th, after the Paduan party had come aboard,
that all the pilgrims were able to register their arrival. Dusk
was falling when at last the *Loredana* sailed.

ADRIATIC VOYAGE

> The fury of the wind drove the galley . . . so that
> the captain himself was not without fear and gave
> orders to strike the mainsail . . . thus they had to
> negotiate the huge waves as best they might . . . the
> pilgrims were so battered that they gave themselves
> up for dead, and not only the pilgrims in the galley
> but the sailors also.
>
> Gabriele Capodilista:
> Itinerario in Terra Santa, 1458

I

The *Loredana* was a trireme, not, however, in the classical
sense of having three banks of oars. Three men pulled on
each oar, claiming the section of the bench on which they
sat as their own private accommodation. The conditions
were very cramped, but food was tolerable and the prospects
of making money were bright. The passengers also were
crowded together; they were not very much better off than
were the crew. The most favoured were allowed to sleep on
the poop, under an awning that protected them from
sun and rain. Experienced pilgrims made certain of berths
on the upper deck, amidships if possible, "for in the lowyst
under it is ryght euyll & smouldryng hote and stynkynge",
as the author of the *Information* so truly said. Four hatch-
ways admitted tenuous streams of light and air into the
long cabin where most of the pilgrims slept, shoulder to
shoulder and toe to toe. The whole lower deck was per-
meated by the loathsome smell of bilgewater; the sand
used as ballast was clammy with it too, and full of decayed

matter left behind or forgotten by earlier travellers. For the pilgrims dug into this gravel with their hands, hiding there eggs and bottles of wine and all their private treasures.

Within, as well as without, the seams of the galley were heavily bedaubed with pitch; in cold weather this was viscous and slimy, in hot sun the tar melted and smeared the pilgrims' clothes with strong-smelling and irremovable stains. The newer galleys could be kept fairly clean by constant scrubbing; by the time they had completed service, which was sometimes as long as twenty years, they had become exceedingly foul. That they were still afloat and still manœuvrable after such a long life was a tribute to the skill and thoroughness of the ship-builders in the Venetian yards. These craftsmen were rightly proud of their work; they continued to lead the Western world for another hundred years. In the end, however, they became victims to their self-satisfaction, for their belief in their technical supremacy was so strong that they were unable to adjust themselves or their methods to new ideas.[1]

The *Loredana*'s predecessor, of the same name, had been commanded by Antonio Loredan's father and uncle.[2] It is known that she carried pilgrims for some fifteen to eighteen years, perhaps longer. The new *Loredana*, modelled closely upon the earlier galley, could carry about the same complement of passengers and crew. In the bow there was a fighting platform, manned by half a dozen *balestrieri*, or cross-bowmen. These, like the ship's officers, were young Venetian patricians, generally younger sons of famous families. Their marksmanship had already been tested at the Arsenal, where regular shooting practice was obligatory for all such youths. They were responsible for the galley's safety, should she be attacked, for it was their business to control and direct the amateurish efforts of the *galeotti*.

At the top of the mainmast was a crow's nest or 'basket' whence the look-out man shouted his observations to the captain and officers. The stern was occupied by a large high

castle, stoutly built and covered with tarred planks to make
it strong and watertight. The captain (Diedo) had his
quarters here, also Antonio Loredan; the most privileged
passengers were sometimes entertained in the castle, as well
as any distinguished guests who might come aboard when
the *Loredana* was in port. At one side of the stern were
lightly built privies, rather like wicker baskets, overhanging
the sea. It is easy to believe that they were difficult if not
impossible to use in bad weather.

Close beside the mainmast, on the upper deck, was the
place of prayer. Here, too, was the 'market' where goods
were sold and bartered by the pilgrims themselves, or by the
galeotti who found they could make a good living by selling
at exorbitant prices merchandise that they bought cheaply
in the various ports. The pilgrims were too ignorant to be
able to find such goods for themselves; they were an easy
prey for the *galeotti* who could persuade or browbeat them
into buying practically anything.

In the *Loredana*, as in most galleys, every pilgrim was
entitled to a limited amount of deck-space where he could
stow the wooden chest that held his belongings. These boxes
had to be lashed tightly, to prevent them from sliding about
to the confusion of both passengers and crew. If not properly
secured they might trip unwary passers-by, particularly
at night, when cries and curses would fill the air. Next
morning the careless owners would certainly be fined by the
patrono. The crew also stowed their gear on deck, there was
nowhere else for it to go. The weight of luggage carried
by officers and men was regulated according to rank, down
to the *galeotti* who were limited to 150 lbs. apiece.[3] This
had to include all the merchandise they hoped to sell, but
they did have the privilege of stowing it beneath the benches
where they sat to row, so that they could guard against the
pilfering from which the passengers suffered if their *patrono*
was weak or careless.

The kitchens were on the poop. Here the ship's cook and

his assistants did their best to carry out Loredan's promise
to provide his passengers with two hot meals a day. He had
also undertaken to supply them with wine and water; these
were supposed to be available on demand. It seems that
Diedo showed considerable enterprise in taking on board
fresh provisions whenever the galley put into port. Nevertheless, the pilgrims complained about their food as fluently
as any schoolboy. Even if they were not forced to consume
the "feble brede, feble wyne, and stynkynge water" described in the *Information* they did become very tired of the
solid ship's biscuit that replaced bread after they had been
at sea for a week or more. This was hard to chew and harder still to digest; even the patient Gabriele Capodilista
remarked that "those who travel in a galley must accustom
themselves to biscuit that is black, meat that is hard and
wine that is thoroughly unpleasant".[4] At mealtimes the
passengers were summoned by a bugle call; they would
stampede towards their tables not caring that those who fell
by the way might be trodden down or rolled overboard. Life
in a galley was not for the infirm, even the strongest suffered
tortures from the congestion, odours, boisterous weather,
cold, heat, sea-sickness and general discomfort.

Roberto and his friends, the Capodilista cousins, and the
English 'milord' dined in a more civilized manner, at the
captain's table. They enjoyed better service, rather more
elbow-room, and congenial companionship. As a soldier
used to the privations of life in camp or on the march,
Sanseverino did not complain overmuch about the ordinary
drawbacks of the voyage, though he had something to say
of the perils from storms and predators. Nor was the Earl
of Worcester a man to stand upon ceremony. He cared very
little for pageantry and outward show, as he afterwards
proved by wandering about Florence unobtrusively in the
guise of an ordinary student. Tiptoft neither sought nor
received any preferential treatment. Not for him the iron-
bound trunks and boxes, the bags of canvas and leather,

the chests, arks, hutches and sacks that were needed to convey the clothes, jewels, armour, and silver plate that Henry Earl of Derby had found necessary on his pilgrimage some sixty years earlier.[5] His only concern was for the vestments his chaplains must take with them for saying Masses on Mount Calvary and elsewhere.

There were a hundred pilgrims in the *Loredana*,[6] while a further ninety-seven sailed in the companion galley.[7] This ship left Venice on the same evening as did the *Loredana*, but passed quickly out of sight; like the *Loredana* she called at the usual ports, reaching Jaffa just twenty-fours hours before Diedo dropped anchor outside the harbour there. William Wey and his party travelled in the second ship, whose name is not recorded. It seems that most of the ultra-montane pilgrims were on board this galley, for Anton Pelchinger (who described himself as 'professor of Tegern-see') would surely have dined and consorted with Gabriele and Antonio Capodilista had he been on board the *Loredana*. The Professor wrote a conventional itinerary of his travels; it is a disappointing book that adds nothing to the narrative. Nowhere does he mention any other pilgrim, even by implication, nor has the Vienna manuscript[8]—that appears to be the only extant copy of this work—any marginal comments to cast light upon the author or his circumstances. A Dutchman, too, wrote a nine-page summary of the journey;[9] presumably he also travelled with William Wey. There were no women in either ship in 1458, although intrepid females did sometimes make the trip either with or without their husbands. The names of twenty-six of the pilgrims in Loredan's party can be discovered by one means or another: they will be found listed in Appendix A.

II

Soon after the last passenger had come aboard, Diedo, Loredan's cousin and now the galley's captain, gave orders for the *Loredana* to slip her moorings. The pilgrims crowded on deck to watch the rowers unship their oars and begin to propel the galley forward with long fluent strokes. The crew now settled down to yet another routine trip to Jaffa. As the sun set on their starboard quarter, in a golden glow, the lights of houses on the Giudecca began to glimmer through the dark. Presently, the breeze freshened a little and the sails filled. Before long the wind blew steadily, so that the oars could be shipped and stowed away beside the benches of the *galeotti*. By morning the ship had travelled nearly fifty miles from the lagoon.

After they had thoroughly explored the ship, the pilgrims did their best to make their quarters tolerable, guarding as best they might against the ravages of rats and cockroaches. Once the first excitement had died down many were at a loss to counter the monotony of their days and nights. The devout and the studious might read devotional books that they had brought from home, or bought from some stall in Venice, as well as they could manage to do so in the dim twilight between decks. Like their fellows on the way to the shrine of St. James at Compostella:

> "Som layde theyr bokys on theyr kne
> And rad so long they myght nat se.
> 'Allas, myne hede wolle cleve on thre!'
> Thus sayth another certayne."[10]

If they crept on deck, trying to find a corner of the poop where they could sit quietly to read in clear daylight, they might be hustled by the sailors and accused of sitting on the ropes or otherwise interfering with the ship's routine. At best they would be elbowed by their more restless fellows; the precious books might be splashed with sea water or even lost overboard.

Some of the more diligent pilgrims started to write notes of all that they had seen or heard; no doubt many diaries were begun that languished and were never finished. Those who had the stamina and determination to keep faithful journals found it necessary to write down events exactly as they happened, day by day, sometimes sitting up at night after all the others had gone to sleep. Both the *Viaggio* of Sanseverino and the *Itinerario* of Capodilista show signs of the conditions in which they were written, small inconsistencies, repetitions, and an occasional error in dating. More remarkable, however, is their very great similarity—it is impossible to believe that during the voyage they were written independently, for in certain passages they are identical in content differing only in their provincial spelling and idiom. It is noticeable that the journals are closest on days when nothing in particular is happening: when the writers go sightseeing on shore their personal interests lead them to record different items, but on their return to the ship the narrative again becomes communal. It is not until the pilgrims reach Jerusalem that these two diaries begin noticeably to diverge; from that point onwards they reveal much more clearly the contrasting characters of the writers, who are thereafter less preoccupied with weather conditions and personal discomfort.

Besides eating, sleeping, reading, writing, betting on the ship's daily run and telling one another stories, most of the pilgrims played simple, childish games. Some contrived to set out chessmen on an improvised board, ignoring as well as they could the jostling of their fellows and the motion of the ship. Problems of personal hygiene, of destroying the vermin that bred so quickly in these crowded conditions, of cleaning and mending clothes and bedding, of renewing equipment and replenishing dwindling stocks of food—all these gave the pilgrims occupation that, although tedious, at least provided them with topics for conversation and grumbling.

The priests among the pilgrims in the *Loredana* said Mass daily for their fellows but, as Sanseverino said: "in the manner in which Mass is said at sea, that is to say without the oblation of the sacrifice".[11] This was known as the *Messa Secca*, or Dry Mass. The Host was neither consecrated nor consumed, for fear of accident and the danger of sea-sickness. In addition, the pilgrims' private devotions took up a considerable part of the day, thus providing a rhythm for the monotony of their existence. Only the bugle blasts that summoned the voyagers to meals divided the long hours. At these signals the general stampede towards the poop was occasioned less by greed or hunger than by a very natural boredom.

The *patrono* recognized that his passengers might well be pining for physical exercise. One day, to celebrate the fact that the *Loredana* had made a record run, he invited the keenest and most athletic of the young men to join the sailors in an acrobatic display. They stood on one another's shoulders to a height level with the top of the mainmast, ascending and descending the rigging hand over hand to the applause of their fellows. Sanseverino wrote warmly of their skill and daring; to Capodilista they seemed "more like monkeys than men, and more like birds than monkeys." After this demonstration it was difficult for the sailors to stop the passengers from climbing the rigging whenever they felt inclined to do so. Some also made a practice of balancing on the gunwale and jumping over the ropes, to the profound annoyance of the crew who were greatly impeded in their work.

III

The coast of Istria had been sighted in the evening of their first day out from Venice. As they passed through the Gulf of Trieste the pilgrims caught a glimpse of various cities illuminated for a moment by the rays of the sun or silhouetted against their contrasting mountain background. The port of Parenzo stood out clearly; pilgrim galleys usually put in here to take on supplies of water and the good local mutton, and to gather fresh herbs for salads;[12] but the *Loredana* held on her course since she was making such good progress. Nor did she put in to Zara, nor the islands of Lesina (Hvar) and Curzola (Korčula) lying off the Dalmatian coast, but pressed on to Ragusa (now Dubrovnik).

When morning broke on Wednesday, May 24th, the pilgrims found themselves within five miles of this port; they prepared with some pleasure to make their first expedition ashore. The galley had already been sighted by the look-out men at the harbour mouth; at once the chief magistrates (or *Signoria*) of Ragusa sent a responsible official, named Ser Bartolomeo dei Sfondrati, to meet the ship. He told Sanseverino and his friends of the arrangements made for their entertainment, greeting them particularly warmly because he himself came from Cremona and was thus a fellow subject of the Duke of Milan. The city Chancellor, David de Bochatij, was also a Lombard; he hailed from Piacenza. Both officials had many questions to ask about affairs in the Duchy; Roberto and his friends were glad to be able to give them news of home. Sfondrati and Bochatij delighted the Milanese by inviting them to spend the night in their homes rather than in the lodgings provided by the *Signoria*.

A civic luncheon party for all the pilgrims proved a stupendous meal. This gave the guests great satisfaction, accompanied as it was by gifts of wine and delicacies. The *Signoria* greeted Paduans as well as Milanese with "a thousand caresses and endearments"; together they made up a party to explore the city. First, the pilgrims examined the palace: to Gabriele "magnificent, with five great towers; from the windows one can see the whole city and the port"; to Roberto "very beautiful, and built in the Venetian style". The trip round the palace completed, everyone accepted refreshment—"una collatione abondatissima di confectione"[13]—before setting out on a conducted tour of the city. They went first to visit the treasury at the church of Our Lady. Here they saw "innumerable relics", including the head, arm and leg of St. Blaise. All these the pilgrims kissed with deep reverence. Never had Roberto observed "such a wealth of silver reliquaries, nor such a profusion of wax candles". Gabriele noted in his diary that the saint's fingers were adorned with his own rings and that the foot still had its full complement of toes.

Almost all the pilgrims now joined the party; together they were led round the walls and shown the beauties of the city and the harbour. Capodilista was fascinated by the great fountain, standing between the churches of S. Francesco and Santa Chiara, with its eight jets of water soaring to a great height, the drops sparkling as they fell. Sanseverino, as might be expected, was more interested in the fortifications. The walls he found were "enormous and very beautiful", being constructed partly from the mountainside, with steps hewn from the rock "as at Gaeta".[14] The next day, after hearing Mass at S. Francesco, Roberto insisted on visiting the walls again, confirming on a second inspection that the fortifications were "inexpugnabile". The rest of the party went sightseeing, much refreshed by the comfortable night they had spent on shore. Towards evening they all met to dine at S. Francesco, where another meal had been prepared for the whole company at the expense of the *Signoria*. Ser Bartolomeo dei Sfondrati further demonstrated his goodwill by making everyone a present of mutton, sweet biscuits, comfits, and many other things to improve their diet and well-being on board the galley.

It was nearly midnight before the pilgrims had finished saying goodbye to the hospitable people of Ragusa; they re-embarked for the next stage with a great sense of well-being. The galley made a very early start next morning; indeed, when the passengers were wakened by the creaking of the oars they found that they were already outside the harbour. There was not a breath of wind; the *galeotti* had to row all day and all night to cover a mere fifteen miles. On Saturday they began to discern the mountains of Albania; the *galeotti* rowed on through the calm till evening fell. The *Loredana* was still making very slow progress, but her passengers were cheered by the sudden appearance of a shoal of "delphini" which the sailors told them always heralded good fortune at sea.

On this occasion, however, the dolphins heralded change rather than good fortune, for on Sunday morning, May 28th, a contrary wind began to blow, increasing in force all that night and the next day. By Tuesday the seas were swelling high; large drops of rain came splashing down. The galley could make no headway as she wallowed in the trough of great waves; the pilgrims were cold and sick, their clothes sodden with rain and spray. Baldessare Diedo had long ago given orders to strike the mainsail and reef the mizzen, but the waves grew larger and larger; at last there was nothing more that he or the sailors could do. "Only by the grace of God was the galley kept afloat that day and that night." According to Capodilista even the *patrono* showed signs of fear. Then Loredan resorted to a gesture familiar to sailors but new to most of the pilgrims. Taking pieces of paper he wrote on them all the saints' names that he could remember, then put the slips into his hat. Selected pilgrims each drew out a slip, read it, and committed the saint's name to memory. Then, each had to vow that he would have a Mass said to that saint in the event of his safe arrival on shore. Finally, all cast their slips of paper into the sea. Roberto da Sanseverino was one of those chosen to draw; either on this occasion, or when the process was repeated on his return journey, he drew the name of Santa Maria di Monte Artone, a famous shrine about eight miles from Padua. Roberto later recorded in his diary that he fulfilled the vow on January 14th, 1459, "at the earliest possible moment after his return".

By evening the pilgrims' prayers had turned from entreaty

to thanksgiving, for quite suddenly the wind dropped, the rain ceased, and the waves abated. Diedo told Sanseverino that he had never known such vile weather or such mighty seas, and many of the sailors bore him out. This was, perhaps, part of their service. Pilgrims liked to look back on terrible dangers narrowly survived; in retrospect these made their whole enterprise seem more meritorious, while a little exaggeration brought colour and interest to the stories they would be able to tell admiring friends and relations when they reached home. As one Harry Stradling wrote to his wife two years earlier: "ther was never man had so perilous a way as we had."[15]

The route now lay along the coast of Albania; the pilgrims had a clear view of the wild and craggy shore backed by high mountains. When at mid-day the port of Durazzo* came into view, Diedo decided that he would put in there to repair his much-buffeted ship. The passengers, too, would be grateful for a chance of rest and quiet; all of them were, as Capodilista said, "lassi et afflicti" after their recent experience. As the *Loredana* turned towards the shore, the pilgrims perceived another galley, also heading for Durazzo. This was the *Contarina*, one of the finest ships that the Venetian yards ever produced. She was commanded by her owner, Don Alessandro Contarini; when the galleys came within a short distance of one another he rowed over in a small boat to come aboard the *Loredana*, since wind and sea were making so much noise that it was impossible for the pilgrims to hear what he had to say. He was able to give them news of the reported death† of Alfonso, King of Aragon, and of the recent advance of the Turks into the Morea. Antonio Loredan asked Contarini if he could let the *Loredana* have a barrel of water and some wood; both of these requirements Contarini was able and willing

* Now Durrës.

† He was very ill at the time but did not actually die until later in the month.

to provide. His "bonissima voglia" extended further than this, for, on Loredan's suggestion, he agreed to lash the two ships together so that they could row with double strength, thus reaching harbour in the teeth of a contrary wind.

The pilgrims were indeed glad to spend a night ashore. As soon as they had disembarked they all set about finding lodgings. Roberto and his friends went with Contarini and the Rector of Durazzo,* who had met them in the harbour with many demonstrations of good will, to the convent of S. Francesco. Here, quarters had been prepared for them. The accommodation, however, did not please Roberto. Complaining that not enough room had been provided for his party, he somewhat ungraciously left his hosts and sought lodgings in S. Domenico. The Dominican brothers received the Milanese most joyfully, offering beds for everyone and providing them with an excellent supper. As in Ragusa, Roberto was deeply interested in examining the walls of the ancient city. He made some notes on the history of Durazzo, spending several hours before supper in a tour of the city's monuments and churches. Capodilista was impressed by the bronze statue of the Emperor Constantine "mounted on horseback, with one arm raised, gazing out to sea":[16] he too admired the triple walls and the ancient battlements; but from a less professional and more aesthetic point of view.

Next morning, Saturday, June 3rd, the pilgrims who had slept in Durazzo attended an early Mass at S. Domenico, for they expected the galley to sail within a few hours' time. Again, a contrary wind prevented their departure, so it was arranged that the pilgrims should wait ashore until the evening. Most of them enjoyed the few hours' respite from the rigours of the voyage. The Rector of Durazzo brought them presents of fruit and resinated wine; when the pilgrims

---

* Niccolò Barbo, member of a famous Venetian family, a kinsman of Cardinal Pietro Barbo who afterwards became Pope Paul II.

returned to the galley two hours before midnight this Messer Niccolò Barbo accompanied them to the quayside in person, in order to cheer them on their way.

A fair wind carried the *Loredana* out of harbour and rapidly along the coast. After passing Corfu a course was laid straight for Candia in Crete. Pilgrim galleys usually called here to take in supplies, but when they arrived, on Wednesday June 7th, they were warned that plague was raging in the city. Roberto and his companions had already disembarked when Antonio Loredan gave orders that nobody was to leave the ship. He peremptorily recalled the Milanese and told them to come aboard immediately. It might have been expected that Roberto would resent the order, but he accepted it without question or comment beyond the terse remark "and so it was done". Nevertheless, on a roll-call of the passengers it turned out that Gabriele and Antonio Capodilista, unaware of Loredan's prohibition, had also already gone ashore. They went to stay with a Venetian friend, a patrician named Tadeo Querini, who owned a beautiful house in Candia. While messengers searched for the cousins, they sat at ease in their host's garden, enjoying his hospitality and the "gentle courtesy and caresses"[17] with which they were received. The truants stayed in Candia for two nights, then returned to the galley quite unconscious of their transgression. They certainly did not contract plague; indeed, on the next stage of their voyage they were almost the only passengers who remained free from sickness. To make sure that no one else could leave the ship Loredan set a close guard, nor would he lie in the harbour but anchored the galley outside.

Early next morning they weighed anchor and set out again, sailing steadily with a following wind. At mid-morning on Saturday, June 10th, the island of Rhodes had just been sighted when a fast-moving ship came into view. As the gap between the two vessels narrowed it became clear that this was no friendly galley to give them the latest news and a barrel of water. She was, indeed, an armed pirate-ship from Genoa. As she approached, the pilgrims were filled with deep foreboding; the *balestrieri* and the *galeotti* began to reach for their weapons. Baldessare Diedo, however, was a captain experienced in the ways of pirates. When the Genoese came within earshot he shouted a warning to them to stand away, declaring that the *Loredana* was a Catalan ship with several cases of plague on board. The pirates were uncertain whether to believe him, but they stood off while they conferred among themselves. In the meantime, Diedo with excellent seamanship had edged the *Loredana* away so that she was soon some distance from her pursuer. The Genoese then sailed off in search of better prey. "Thus, by the grace of God, by the strength of the sails, and the astuteness of the sailors, we escaped from their impious hands." as Roberto wrote in his *Viaggio* that night.

5

THE ISLAND OF RHODES

When the galley was fastened in the port with cables,
the pilgrims . . . went on land to refresh their bodies
and visit friends, because at Rhodes, amongst the
brethren of St. John of Jerusalem, there are natives
of many countries.

Canon Pietro Casola's Pilgrimage, 1494

On leaving Candia the *Loredana* made fitful progress
towards her next port of call. "Now by the wind in the sails
and now by the force of the oars they passed through many
shoals; all that night they continued in this manner,"
wrote Gabriele Capodilista in his quiet and careful narrative.
He estimated that they had covered nearly ninety miles
since Crete, but that much of this distance had been lost
by a navigational error. Gabriele kept his own chart; he
traced out their progress very accurately, demonstrating
to Diedo that his mistaken reckoning had set the galley
many miles off her proper course. They were, in fact, heading northwards instead of east. If they were to visit Rhodes,
as they had planned, the galley would have to pick her way
through a string of islands where there were dangerous
shoals and currents. Gabriele feared it might even be necessary to jettison some of the *Loredana*'s cargo. As this would
certainly mean that the passengers' baggage would have to
be sacrificed, the amateur navigator was far from popular
with his fellow pilgrims. However, "by the grace of God
and the prudence of the sailors", all was well. The gusty
wind dropped to a light steady breeze from the desired
quarter, while the helmsman negotiated all the hazards

successfully. This unsought advice might have meant some tension between Capodilista and the acting *patrono*, had not both men been intelligent and magnanimous. No one could be angry with Gabriele Capodilista for long, for his modest and charming manners conquered everyone.

The welcome they received on arrival at Rhodes compensated the pilgrims for all their privations and alarms. All had looked forward to a real holiday in this hospitable island, where men from so many nations were gathered. It was one of the provisions in Loredan's contract that the galley must not remain in any one port for more than six days; had it been otherwise many of his passengers might have chosen to stay at Rhodes for several weeks.

The first boat to put out from shore, as the *Loredana* dropped anchor in the harbour, was "una barcha" sent by the Patriarch of Aquileia for the transport of the Capodilista cousins. The Patriarch was the Cardinal Luigi Scarampo, a large florid man who was more of a sailor than an ecclesiastic. In the summer of 1458 he was organizing the defence of Rhodes against attack by Turkish vessels, for this was the dark cloud hanging over the island. However massive the fortifications, however indomitable the defenders, the Knights knew how vulnerable Rhodes was to a surprise attack, for they could not depend upon the loyalty of the population—so mixed and varied were the races. As a person, Scarampo was attractive, witty, and artistic; he possessed a true Venetian's love of beauty and splendour. Moreover, he was massively rich. It was said that only Cosimo de' Medici had greater resources; certainly Scarampo made his money talk much more loudly than did the grave Florentine. He had used his Eastern connection to secure rich oriental furnishings for his great house near Rome,[1] where the hangings tinkled with sequins and the gardens were full of exotic animals and birds. Although Scarampo was only residing temporarily in Rhodes, the luxury of his apartments there was already famous, as was his hospitality. He was an old friend of Gabriele and Antonio, as anxious as they were to renew their companionship. The cousins set off at once; they were established as honoured guests in the Patriarch's house before anyone else had succeeded in reaching the quay.

Without waiting for the rest of the passengers to disembark, the *galeotti* scrambled ashore as soon as the galley was made fast, taking with them the merchandise they had brought from Venice. As was customary, they set up stalls near the harbour, holding a sort of fair for the islanders. The seamen sold their own goods at a high price; they also made shrewd purchases of things—mainly food and drink —that they believed they would be able to sell profitably to the passengers.

Every pilgrim was determined to land, to see the sights, to buy necessities, and above all to stretch his cramped limbs. A few saved money by continuing to sleep aboard the galley, satisfying themselves by wandering through the streets during the daytime. Most, however, preferred to find lodgings where they could extend their arms and legs without buffeting their sleeping neighbours, and where their own slumbers would not be disturbed by rats. Sanseverino and the other Milanese received a message from a Knight of their acquaintance² that the 'House of Santa Caterina' had been reserved for them and their servants for the duration of their visit. On this occasion Roberto found everything to his liking, so his party slept there with great satisfaction as long as the galley remained in port.

Next day, a Sunday,* the Patriarch announced that he was preparing a supper party for the Paduans. He invited also Roberto and his friends, nor did he forget the Englishman, John Earl of Worcester. John Tiptoft now came into his own, for it turned out that the Castellan was himself an Englishman, as were several of the Knights. They made much of Tiptoft, who showed himself in his most gracious

* June 11th.

light. The Castellan—whose name is not recorded— resolved to provide a feast next day in honour of his country- man.

It is difficult to establish exactly how many Knights of Rhodes there were at this time; most of them were French with a sprinkling of Spaniards, Italians, and Portuguese. Englishmen and Germans were in a small minority. At a grand review, held on the island sixty-four years later, it seems that two hundred and ninety-five Knights paraded.[3] As the numbers diminished somewhat during the two generations following Sanseverino's visit in 1458 there must have been more than three hundred of them. These Knights Hospitallers, or Knights of St. John, had originally been a military order designed to form a bodyguard for pilgrims travelling to and from the Holy Land. It is true that they still had skirmishes with their hereditary enemies, the Ottoman Turks, but by the fifteenth century they had become much less martial. Their interest in pilgrims' welfare continued; they still ran their excellent hospital for the sick and injured, but they concentrated less upon protection than upon hospitality. Entertaining pilgrims of their own social standing was their special pleasure; they also carried out their duty of helping them to solve all problems incidental to a long and tedious voyage. Their spirit as well as their power was diminishing; the time was not so very far distant when their headquarters would be transferred to Malta,* and the islands they owned would come under Turkish rule.

At daybreak most of the pilgrims attended Mass at Santa Caterina. As they emerged from the church they found horses waiting for them, brought by a number of Knights who had come to conduct the visitors to the Grand Master. He, poor man, lay miserably in bed, nursing an attack of gout, nevertheless he had sent a message that he

* In 1522 the Grand Master was defeated by the Turks and fled to Candia. Three years later the Emperor Charles V granted the Knights lands in Malta, where they became permanently established.

wished to speak with Roberto da Sanseverino in order to assure him of his good will and his affection for the Duke of Milan. This invitation seemed to Roberto an excellent opportunity to further his uncle's interests. He had already written to Sforza a brief letter, as soon as he arrived, telling him such items of news as he had been able to gather concerning the Turks, though these did not amount to very much. He added that he would write more fully at a later date. As, indeed, he did.

The Grand Master at this time was a Frenchman, Jacques de Milly. After their talk he told Roberto that he had made arrangements for him to be conducted round the walls and fortifications; also, if he so wished, he could see the Hospital and, of course, the Treasury. It was at the Hospital that Sanseverino rejoined the other pilgrims; they were examining its conduct with deep interest. There was nothing else quite like it in their experience. Patients of all nationalities and creeds were received in the Hospital, treated for their ailments, and fed most lavishly. The actual work of nursing was done by paid orderlies under the supervision of two surgeons and two physicians. The sick were examined twice daily, the doctors supplying from a well-stocked dispensary any drugs that they deemed necessary. The Knights visited the patients regularly, comforting them with conversation backed by presents of wine from their famous cellar. Some of the rules, however, seemed to Capodilista somewhat harsh, for the sufferers were permitted to read only devotional books; neither chronicles nor romances had a place in the library. Nor were patients allowed to play games of chess or draughts.

Before supper there was just time to inspect the Arsenal, and to examine the munitions stored for use in the war galleys. Roberto was, as ever, deeply interested in the war machines. With the Earl of Worcester, who shared his regard for weapons, Roberto examined with admiration certain *balestre* that were able to throw enormous arrows.

After the meal was over, when the pilgrims were content to sit on comfortable cushions digesting the rich food while they ruminated over the day's happenings, they discovered that further entertainment had been planned for them. In the house of a Greek citizen—the majority of the citizens of Rhodes were Greeks—they watched a display of Greek dancing, delighted to find that the steps and movements were fundamentally similar to the Italian style that they knew so well. "It was a pleasant ending to the day," wrote Roberto, the pilgrims receiving "loving greetings and much honour from all the men and women who were present".[4]

On returning to their lodgings the Milanese found that a note had been delivered there, containing a further invitation. The English Castellan asked them to a dinner party the next day, to be held in his private garden a few miles outside the city. Accordingly at ten o'clock in the morning, the Milanese, the Paduans, and of course John Tiptoft in whose honour the banquet was being held, set out on horseback. The Castellan himself, with a large number of the Knights, had ridden out to meet them. As they passed through the olive groves, the air was heavy with the scent of sweet herbs crushed beneath the horses' hooves. They found the garden spread over a wide area; it was full of "beautiful tall trees, mainly cedars and chestnuts, with thickets of bay laurel, and orange groves set with ornamental fountains". Everywhere there was fruit "in luscious profusion", with cool shade and greenness to rest the pilgrims' eyes after the glitter of the waves and the reflection from hot sun striking on the deck. Dinner was laid on low tables set in the shade, with rich carpets laid over the bushes or suspended from the trees. Everywhere hung garlands of the most fragrant flowers. The repast itself was delicious and succulent, each of the many courses accompanied by resinous local wines. Small wonder that the guests were content to lie back and enjoy complete relaxation in this peaceful garden, so completely free from the noise, squalor and stench that had assailed them in their ship.

Although the catering standards of the *Loredana* were comparatively high, the food on board was bound to be monotonous and stale. That is why the diarists dwelt at such length upon the occasional feasts that came their way. Sanseverino had the strongest views on good living and expressed them freely. His delight in the food and wine was frank and honest, like the man himself; this dinner party was for Roberto one of the highlights of his voyage.

After their siesta the party again visited the Castello, where Roberto made a further inspection of the Armoury. Next, they were shown relics of S. Antonio and Santa Caterina;* finally, they went to see the most precious treasure of all—a 'spina' from the Crown of Thorns. It was housed in a tabernacle of crystal and silver, most marvellously wrought. This Holy Thorn was reported to flower each year upon Good Friday and to remain in bloom from the sixth hour to the ninth. Not only the Knights but all the people of Rhodes testified to this miracle; Roberto and his companions were assured by many people that they had witnessed it themselves. The rest of the evening was spent in bidding goodbye to their friends and in thanking them for the "elegant hospitality" the pilgrims had enjoyed.

Early next morning, a light dawn breeze blowing, they clambered aboard the galley. Soon they were gliding along, greatly cheered by their many presents of fruit and wine and the good wishes of their kind hosts. As Rhodes faded out of view one final incident rounded off this most pleasant of their experiences. It is recorded by both diarists: a flash of colour in their matter-of-fact pages. A bird was seen flying in the wake of the ship; presently it flew aboard and settled in the rigging. It was the most beautiful creature that any of them had ever seen, marked with every colour of

* Of Alexandria. Caterina Benincasa of Siena was not yet canonized.

the rainbow. Since Roberto says that it was "about the size of a starling" perhaps it was a bee-eater.* Fatigue had made the bird so tame that it was easily caught and handled; after resting some time in the rigging it recovered and flew away, its brilliance no more than a memory. Everyone was pleased by the incident except those of the *galeotti* who had planned to put it in their stew.

* *Merops apiaster.*

6

CYPRUS TO THE HOLY LAND

The Kingdom of Cyprus is for the most part
unhealthy . . . As I was going along I was seized
with such terrible pains in my head that I thought
I was about to die. The pain descended to my legs
and attacked the stomach, the belly, hips, thighs and
the knees down to the feet, and it lasted all that
night and the following day until Vespers.

Pero Tafur: *Travels & Adventures*, 1435-9[1]

I

Light winds slowed down the *Loredana*'s progress, the sun
beating unremittingly on deck as she dawdled through the
sparkling water. It was not until late in the evening of
Thursday, June 15th, that the look-out man was able to
cry that he had sighted Cyprus. When they awoke next
morning the pilgrims found themselves close inshore; by
two o'clock they had reached "Baffo",* a town that Roberto
described as "situated on the sea shore, in a ruinous condition and almost uninhabited".[2] Some hours later the galley
put into port near "a little castle named Episcopia" (Episkopi). This belonged to a rich Venetian who had been
banished to Cyprus by the Signoria of Venice. He was
Andrea Cornaro, member of an important patrician family.[3]
The foundations of the Cornaro fortunes were the sugar
plantations spread over a large area between Episkopi and
Limasol, for sugar cane was the most important crop grown
in Cyprus throughout the fifteenth century; it had been

* Presumably, Paphos.

cultivated and processed for the Venetian market ever since the fall of the Latin kingdom of Jerusalem. The Venetians were glad enough to do business with Andrea Cornaro; they did not like his politics, but they needed his cane sugar.

Most of the pilgrims landed at Limasol, intent upon shopping for necessities that were beginning to run very short as the voyage neared its end. Roberto and his companions went straight to the castle at Episkopi to call upon Cornaro. They found his living quarters "very sumptuous", his hospitality lavish. Cornaro entertained his guests with delicious fruits gathered from his garden and orange groves. Roberto noticed the trees loaded with carob beans, "fruits that were long and narrow, bitter-tasting when they were green but as they ripened till nearly black developing a certain sweetness". Most of his praises are reserved for the bananas that he found growing in great profusion; their flavour delighted him and he was pleased to find that "cut them as often as you will, always you will find a cross in the centre of the fruit".*

As many as four hundred men were employed in Cornaro's sugar plantations, every worker receiving his weekly wage on Saturdays.[4] Their produce was graded, packed, and distributed throughout the island as well as overseas. Although Limasol as a city was practically deserted, the port installations remained. The *Loredana* lay safely at anchor there, among the small merchantmen used by Cornaro for transporting his sugar. This commercially minded Venetian was something of a tycoon; he certainly used his banishment to good purpose in amassing a fortune that compared favourably with the possessions and credit of any trader on the mainland. He seems to have borne the Senate no ill will and was as eager to hear news of Venice as to impart to his visitors the local gossip of the island. Among other things, Cornaro told the Milanese

* This fanciful idea was not Roberto's own, it is often found in pilgrims' narratives.

of the recent death of Helena[5] the Queen of Cyprus, second wife of King John II and mother of his only legitimate child.

Gabriele Capodilista, with a dozen companions including his personal servant Tomaso, also visited the plantations and Cornaro's gardens. They set off on mules before sunrise on Saturday, June 17th, in the cool air of early dawn. This party also noted the carob trees, the cedars, and the bananas. These last reminded Gabriele of "little cucumbers, except that they turn yellow when they are ripe."[6] The irrigation of the plantations and the system of rivulets trained to run through the gardens also interested Gabriele; he had a countryman's eye for such matters. Nevertheless, he shared the general view that the climate of Episkopi was atrocious —"pessima", he said. He blamed the "pestilential air" of the island for an epidemic that struck down most of the pilgrims and many of the crew. Even those who had remained aboard the galley suffered from high fever and— according to William Wey—"a bloody flux". After they had sailed away from Cyprus, over a darkening sea with a freshening wind, the pitching of the galley made the sick men still more wretched. Gabriele himself escaped the infection, but his cousin Antonio suffered severely from stomach pains, as did many others among the invalids. The sickness lasted fifteen days or more; Gabriele records that "certain of the pilgrims died", although he does not state how many nor does he mention any of them by name.

The death of a pilgrim here and there was a matter for little comment. At the turn of the century a Scottish archbishop* chartered a ship for himself and his retinue, setting off for Jerusalem in great style and with public acclaim.[7] When, however, the captain brought his ship back to Venice, with only three or four survivors aboard, his statement that the Archbishop and all the others were dead caused little excitement and only a passing notice in the records. That it was quite a common thing for a pilgrim to die during

* Robert Blackader, Archbishop of Glasgow.

the voyage is shown by the clause generally included in the contract between *patrono* and passenger, an agreement that any person who fell ill should have better quarters assigned to him and the services of the ship's doctor (if one were carried). Should he die, the *patrono* would have to return part of the passage money and hand over all the dead man's possessions to his friends. The corpse must be carried to the nearest port: the *patrono* might bury it at sea only if the ship were out of sight of land.

Those who died in the course of a pilgrimage—there must have been far more of these than the individuals whose death was so casually recorded by their fellows—believed themselves certain of salvation. This may have encouraged some who were old and infirm to undertake the risk of making pilgrimage, but the captains of the Venetian galleys were entitled to refuse passages to those obviously unfit to make the voyage. It was a difficult choice to make, for every *patrono*, from a natural desire to take the maximum amount in fares, wanted to carry his full complement of passengers. Yet, those who pined and died brought his galley a bad name; however faithfully he had tended* the pilgrims there would always be mischief-makers ready to claim that he had starved or neglected them. Like most sailors, the *galeotti* were intensely superstitious: to them a death on board ship was always unlucky and might be an omen of disaster; they might 'down oars' at a critical point or refuse to return from shore leave. On the whole the *patroni* preferred to exercise their right to refuse to carry invalids or anyone else they feared might become a liability.

Despite the storm that had blown her off course and the few hours' anxiety when she was intercepted by the Genoese pirate, the *Loredana* had made a satisfactory voyage so far. Nevertheless, the last stage of the sea-trip proved as trying as the experienced *patrono* expected it to be. Those who were ill almost gave up hope, the convalescents were impatient

* Or, as most contracts said, 'cherished'.

and querulous, and even those of unwavering faith felt that the journey was far longer than they had expected. Everyone longed for his first sight of the Holy Land; many times hopes were raised only to be dashed. At last, on Monday, June 19th, at ten o'clock in the morning, came the great moment for which all the pilgrims had been waiting. The mountains of Palestine came suddenly into view, with Mount Carmel standing up sharp and clear. "With one accord they fell upon their knees and sang a *Te Deum laudamus*." When at last the port of Jaffa came into sight, the pilgrims' excitement reached fever-pitch. The sick men struggled from their beds, others shouted and flung their caps into the air, while the many priests who were on board conducted their devotions with renewed zeal, preaching a series of topical sermons in which they advocated "thanksgiving, courage, and moderation".

II

All these qualities were needed, and more beside, before the pilgrims were able to set foot on shore. Baldessare Diedo rounded off his command, before giving up his authority to Loredan, the true *patrono*, by casting anchor about a mile outside the harbour. The pilgrims would have to wait until the required permits and safe-conduct could be obtained from the port officials. Further, a messenger must be sent to Ramleh and on to Jerusalem to make arrangements with the Moorish Governor. He would also have to secure the co-operation of the Franciscan Brothers of Mount Syon, who supervised all Christian pilgrims as long as they stayed in the Holy Land. The second galley having already arrived, Loredan sent his son Niccolò to consult her *patrono* before initiating these negotiations.

Jaffa was a bad harbour at the best of times, being very shallow. Since there was always the danger that the anchor might drag and the galley be driven ashore, the captains

were anxious to land their passengers without delay. As for
the pilgrims, they were loud in their criticism of the arrangements made for their welfare. They no longer felt exalted
by the prospect before them; the emotion inspired by their
first sight of the Holy Land had quickly worn off, to be
replaced by impatience and intolerance of the formalities.
When news was brought that a band of about a hundred
hostile Arabs had attacked a party between Ramleh and
Jaffa—killing two Franciscan friars who were on their
way to Famagusta—the more timorous pilgrims regretted
that they had ever set out; according to Roberto the air
was filled with their lamentations.[8] His own thoughts were
centred on the galley's armoury; the weapons designed for
protection against pirates could well be adapted, he thought,
by the pilgrims for their own defence. "If everyone carried
his arms with valour," he wrote, "there would be no need
for anyone to have fear." To his great disgust, Roberto
found that this was impossible because no pilgrim was
allowed to carry arms of any kind without special permission
from the Governor of Jerusalem. When it turned out that
the death of the friars was a false rumour—they had been
robbed and beaten but were still alive—this news did little
to quiet his growing exasperation. The other pilgrims, however, grew calmer and more resigned; some even seemed
"lieti et contenti". The Paduan cousins and the convalescents
were philosophical enough, resting quietly on their beds,
but Roberto and other men of action found the delay very
hard to bear.

Next morning all the pilgrims were up before daybreak,
crowding on deck to be ready for the signal to land. The
port officials, however, would not be hurried; they break-
fasted in a leisurely manner, giving the pilgrims no intima-
tion as to whether or no their permits had arrived. Antonio
Loredan was accustomed to the dilatory character of the
customs officials and the clerks in the shipping offices:
he knew from long experience just how and when a timely

bribe would yield good results. This was part of his service, for the fare paid by each passenger was said to be inclusive of all tolls and gratuities. Anyone who wished for preferential treatment was free to buy it if he so desired, but most were content to allow their leader to carry out any bribery that might be necessary. They thought, rightly, that he would obtain better value.

While they waited, the nobles of the party took the opportunity to stow away their good clothes and to borrow dirty or ragged garments from their servants. They wished to appear poor and unkempt less from devotion to the pilgrim's ideal—the feeling that it was right and fitting to show humility when visiting the Holy Places—than from expediency. Roberto makes it clear that he put on coarse clothes only in order to evade the extra tolls imposed on those of gentle birth: in the *Viaggio*[9] he alleges that the Saracens took delight in maltreating Christian noblemen and extorting from them illegal tribute. "Indeed, those pilgrims who were great gentlemen or lords clad themselves in garments so villainous that they could not be recognized . . . moreover they parted company from their fellows and associated on equal terms with their own servants so that the Saracens were not able to identify them." This seemed to Roberto a matter for great chagrin; it meant less to the Earl of Worcester who was always at ease with simple people—he found little difficulty in mixing with his servants and chaplains. Gabriele Capodilista had no more to say than that it was "convenient"[10] for master and servants to be dressed alike. Sanseverino had to comfort himself by remarking that, however obtuse the Saracens might be, no man of breeding "however old and strange his apparel" would be able to conceal his quality from his own countrymen.

At last Niccolò Loredan returned from his mission, all arrangements duly made. There were still, however, some formalities to be completed before the pilgrims could be allowed ashore. Each was given a card or ticket with his name and status inscribed upon it; this he would have to carry with him wherever he went and produce it on request. Should he mislay or lose his identity card there would certainly be a fine to pay; if he were a man of some importance it might cost him a large sum to get it replaced. Poorer pilgrims were not much troubled by officialdom, for the excellent reason that they were not worth plundering.

By now it was nearly dinner time. Still simmering with impatience the party took their last meal on board ship and began to jostle one another to take up a position for quick disembarkation. Their baggage was fastened and neatly stacked ready to hand; all the flasks had been filled. Experienced pilgrims were already holding in their hands the wooden stirrups that would make so much difference to their comfort when astride primitive saddles poised on the sharp backs of the donkeys. After they had gathered up the last of their possessions and had tipped the ship's officers, word came that they could now go ashore.

The whole party climbed into small boats, or jumped into the surf and struggled to land in their enthusiasm to kiss the sacred ground. There was much crowding and pushing, everyone milling around the gangway, but to very little purpose. Those who hoped by their impetuosity to secure for themselves the best donkeys for the ride to Ramleh were disappointed, for the donkey-boys would not bring their animals until the following morning. This was a fact well known to the more seasoned travellers, who stood back from the unseemly scramble, while they concentrated their own efforts upon alleviating what they knew must be a night of misery.

Every pilgrim, rich or poor, servant or master, was compelled to spend the first night ashore in a dank cave on the beach, stale from the presence of previous visitors, deep in filth and litter that had to be scraped away before it was possible to lie down to rest. The dripping of the roof added further to their discomfort. For the privilege of entering "this vile and stinking place", a tribute of one penny a head was demanded, while an armed guard stood at the mouth of the cave to make sure that no one came out before morning, when he would demand another unauthorized fee to let the pilgrims go. He might, they were told, be bribed to let them out one by one during the night to relieve nature; the pilgrims seem to have resented this imposition even more than the payment of the illegal tolls.

Native traders came, as evening fell, to offer the pilgrims their wares. There were highly priced rushes and branches of shrubby trees to make bedding on the clammy floor. Large sums were asked, too, for water and eggs and lettuces, and the hot cakes displayed to tempt the pilgrims' appetites. Many were so disgusted with the conditions that they were quite unable to eat. Those who could afford it bought perfumes and frankincense, balsam and musk—even attar of roses from Damascus—in an effort to mitigate the powerful smells, but most people had to lie like cattle in discomfort and misery. Everything that happened after this seemed less harsh by comparison; if any began to grumble at the dirt or roughness of their lodgings hereafter, they were reminded by their fellows of the wretchedness of this first night ashore.

The pilgrims should have been warned by the experience of their predecessors—nearly everyone who wrote an account of his journey to Palestine described vividly and in detail the horrors of these caves, blaming Muslim rapacity for all the frustration and delay in starting towards the climax of their journey. After the unquiet night dawn broke at last. Soon afterwards the donkeys were brought down to the beach. At once there was a wild stampede to secure the best and strongest animals, for every pilgrim knew that all cost the same.* All the guide-books recommended this course, but more thoughtful pilgrims, who

* This 'transport' was part of the inclusive fare.

resented being jostled by the crowd, quietly addressed themselves to the owners. For a small tip these more sophisticated travellers found themselves in possession of the best donkeys and the most obliging 'asse-men'. Intelligent pilgrims made friends with the beasts they were to ride as well as with their drivers; a German Dominican friar[11] had such good fortune with the little black donkey he rode on his first pilgrimage that on his second journey he made great efforts to secure the same animal again, having brought for the 'asse-man' who owned it a present of a pair of iron stirrups all the way from Ulm.

The Milanese party soon found out that the 'asse-men' or donkey boys could be very recalcitrant if they were not courteously treated. Within a few hours Roberto was exclaiming at their "insolence"; on the first morning he had an altercation with the donkey boys that lost the whole party three hours of valuable time. The boys remained obdurate; Roberto had to endure defeat and considerable loss of face. He repeated this mistake on other occasions; it was not until he was travelling in the desert, unaccompanied by his friends, that Roberto learned not to interfere with the regimen of camels or asses. It is noticeable that less is heard in the latter part of the *Viaggio* concerning the rapacity of his drivers, and far more of their efficiency.

In the meantime, the guardians and officials of Ramleh had been placated by presents of wine and wax and wood, brought in his galley for that purpose by Antonio Loredan ("as is the ill custom", commented Sanseverino). In return, they gave gracious permission for the party to spend the night at Ramleh, ten miles from Jaffa. On arrival here, the pilgrims were delighted to find everything arranged for their comfort, even hot baths in splendid marble bathrooms. The Saracens allowed them to hire sleeping mats and to buy provisions for their supper. Wey remarked on the roast fowls, freshly baked bread, and fruit of many kinds, brought to them by local traders. After a good meal and a long sleep everyone had revived sufficiently to rise an hour before dawn. They heard Mass, listening attentively to the long sermon, then, mounting their donkeys or walking barefoot to show their piety and devotion, the pilgrims set out to inspect the first of their Holy Places.

III

The sermon the pilgrims had heard before leaving Ramleh was not only long; it was full of detailed information about the antiquities they were to see, coupled with advice as to suitable behaviour. The Franciscan friar from Mount Syon who preached on this occasion had lived long enough in the Holy Land to understand very well the customs and prejudices of the Saracens, but he had not forgotten the point of view of European visitors. He was, therefore, in the right position to give them practical help in solving their problems.

First, the preacher told the pilgrims that they must constantly show Christian charity, forbearance and tact. They must at all times use towards the Muslims the tolerance that they expected to receive. He added that they must be careful to avoid aggression; never in any way must they offend their hosts. On no account were they to defile Muslim graves by stepping over them, nor should they attempt to enter a mosque. It was unwise to make solitary expeditions; within reason pilgrims could ramble about at will, but they should remain within earshot of their own party. They must always conform to the plans laid down by their leader.

Further exhortations of the Franciscan preacher were reported by William Wey in his *Itineraries*. Some of them throw light upon the manners of certain types of pilgrim and show why it was that they sometimes excited anger and indignation. It was becoming customary for foreigners who happened to be of noble birth to set up their coats of arms in their lodgings—this is seen particularly in the universities where foreign students carved or painted their shields on wall or ceiling as a record of their sojourn. These shields—as, for instance, in the *cortile* of the University at Padua, or the Archiginnasio at Bologna—were often very decorative. Such records are interesting to posterity, but it is easy to see how offensive the practice might be to contemporary people of an alien civilization. For pilgrims to set up coats of arms—often with Christian emblems—on the walls of places in the Holy Land where they had been shown hospitality was thought by their hosts to be the height of arrogance.

Then, as now, pilgrims seem to have had a strong desire to carve their names or initials on shrines that they visited. Graffiti, scrawled in red lead, can indeed still be discerned at the entrance to the church and on the columns of the north side of the Holy Sepulchre. This habit was condemned by the preacher in the strongest terms, as was the still more reprehensible practice of taking home as souvenirs stones and fragments from the Holy Places. There had even been some, the friar told his congregation, who had not hesitated to chip pieces from the Holy Sepulchre itself. These admonitions and prohibitions were carefully listed by William Wey in his précis of the friar's sermon. It is the more regrettable that on a fly-leaf of his *Itineraries* there is written—perhaps in his own hand—an inventory of the relics that he himself brought home from Palestine. Among them were:

"a ston of the Mownte of Calvery
a stone of Sepulkyr
a stone of the hyl of Tabor
a stone of the pyler that ovre Lord was stowrchyd toc
a stone of the plas wher the crorse was hyd and funde
also a stone of the holy cave of Bethlem."[12]

All these he placed in a reliquary and, together with hi⸱

map of the Holy Land "wyth Jerusalem in the mydds",
he presented them to his convent at Edington.

Had all pilgrims been as acquisitive as Wey it is easy to
see that there would soon have been no Holy Places left
to visit.

IN AND ABOUT JERUSALEM

> At Betany in an old castel
> Ys Lazarys tombe made full wele:
> Also at Betany ys a stone
> Aroun whyche Martha knelyd [d]own,
> And seyd to Cryst, w/t mylde chere,
> My brother had not dyed and ye had be here.
> *The Itineraries of William Wey*, 1458

I

William Wey's doggerel verses* were devised for the one purpose of helping pilgrims to memorize the sequence of Holy Places and their associations. The point was to make sure that no important shrine had been omitted from the itinerary. It was the easiest thing in the world, where so many items had to be remembered, to overlook one or two that seemed at the time unimportant but that in retrospect proved to be very grave omissions. Wey's verses were probably much more helpful than the academic instructions contained in most guide-books, though these laboriously hand-written lists were useful, too, for their calendars of prescribed devotions at every point. Bemused pilgrims, their minds occupied by totting up the indulgences they were gaining, and the genuine efforts they were making to concentrate upon the recital of their prayers, were in no condition for sightseeing with a fresh and observant eye. For the most part they flocked from point to point,

* He was, perhaps, quoting the poem from some earlier pilgrim book; normally he preferred a terse and business-like prose style.

obedient to their leader, oblivious of the life going on around them and unaware of the strange civilization through which they were passing. Even the normal observances proved too exacting for the human frailty of the slower witted or the less energetic. So much had to be crowded into so few days that it is not surprising that homeward-bound pilgrims often found that important items had been unaccountably omitted from their carefully planned tour. Even Wey, ardent explorer that he was, felt himself obliged to make a second pilgrimage, four years later, in order to revisit all the stations and to resolve eleven 'doubts' concerning the antiquities and traditions of Jerusalem.

Armed with Wey's guide-book it should have been a simple matter for the pilgrim to find his way from one site to another, for the Holy Places were grouped into convenient daily expeditions—'Pylgrymages in the Vale of Syloe', 'of Mount Syon', 'of Bethlehem' and so on. Distances were approximate, but near enough to give the sightseers a practical idea of what they were undertaking. Then, as now, tourists had to be content to entrust the organization of the tour to their leader while they suspended—for the common good—independence of mind and action. Only occasionally was divergence from the normal schedule permitted, for it was liable to throw the whole programme into confusion and might spoil everyone's satisfaction.

II

Roberto and his companions had lingered at Ramleh for an extra day, beguiled by the unexpected luxury of their quarters after the misery of their first night ashore. Their only activity was a short excursion to Lydda, two or three miles away, in order to visit the shrine marking the site of the martyrdom of St. George. Some said this was also the place where he slew the dragon; others believed the scene of this famous conflict to be Beirut. Dismounting from their donkeys, the pilgrims went on foot to inspect the church. One by one they knelt to kiss the block of stone on which the saint's head had been severed from his body, then, looking around them, they were shocked to see that the whole building was in ruinous condition. Roberto noted that "the church had once been very beautiful",[1] contrasting it sadly with the splendid mosque that stood nearby. During the cool of the evening the pilgrims returned to Ramleh in thoughtful mood, musing on the associations of the first of the Holy Places they had visited.

To have spent further time at Ramleh would have meant reducing the number of sightseeing days in Jerusalem and its environs. It was already June 23rd; the pilgrims were still a day's journey from the Holy City. By July 4th at the latest they must be back at Jaffa. Thus, only eleven days remained for their tour, a short allowance for an expedition that was generally reckoned to take a fortnight. The briefest recorded time for a pilgrimage that included all the standard items was nine days;[2] those parties preferring to work at lower pressure found three weeks barely sufficed for all they wanted to see and do.

Next morning the pilgrims set out for Jerusalem some three hours late, on account of Roberto's "alterchatione" with the donkey-boys. They therefore had to travel at speed over a road that they found both stony and difficult. As though to emphasize that they were in a strange land, a cavalcade of Muslims came riding towards them, with a military band of pipes and drums, the brown-faced Moors clad in brilliantly coloured garments and riding splendid horses.[3] They were acting as escort to the Emir of Jerusalem, who was on his way to Ramleh. They took no notice of the pilgrims, who plodded on through country that Roberto described as "mountainous, rocky, and very depressing". Many were hurt by falling pebbles that came bouncing down from the hillside on either hand. After about thirteen miles of this uncomfortable progress the pilgrims were glad to dismount beside a bubbling spring, near some olive trees and the ruined walls of an ancient castle, that promised refreshment and shade from the sun's fierce rays. Here they dined and took a short rest, for they were now travelling in the heat of the day. Everyone felt clammy with sweat; many of the pilgrims had become querulous or pettish, others "made a dismal complaining". It was certainly time they had a rest.

Soon, their spirits revived. Leaving their little oasis the party were again on their way. They even felt strong enough to turn aside, visiting first Emmaus, "where the two disciples knew Our Lord Jesus in the breaking of bread", and then Arimathea, birthplace of Joseph and the tomb of the prophet Samuel. The pilgrims were not allowed to linger here, for it was necessary to hurry if they wished to reach Jerusalem before nightfall. When at last they stumbled up to the top of Mount Joy, a prospect of the city lay before them, with a clear view also of the Mount of Olives. All fell on their knees, their tribulations forgotten in a glow of religious fervour. Bruises and blisters did not matter any more; for the rest of the way they pressed on resolutely, entering Jerusalem just before ten o'clock that night.

So eager were they to visit the Holy Sepulchre without delay that Roberto and the other Milanese made their way thither, disregarding their leader's instructions to wait until morning. But when they arrived in the forecourt they found that the church was shut. Nor could they discover anyone with authority to open the great door. In a very ill temper the pilgrims had to return to the lodging provided for them in the Hospital of St. John, that they had not yet inspected. Roberto was determined to find fault. He said that the rooms were unsuitable and too small—"molto inepto et guasto"[4] were his words. His servants were dispatched to seek fresh quarters, but since it was by this time late at night, they could find nothing acceptable. At last the Milanese called upon the Franciscan Brothers of Mount Syon.* It was not, at this time, usual for laymen to stay in the monastery; it is doubtful if they would have been allowed to do so, had it not been for the intervention of Fra Francesco of Brescia. More resourceful than truthful, the friar (who recognized Roberto as a fellow countryman) claimed him as his own "brother of the flesh" with the utmost assurance, and "in a loud voice" begged for his admission; indeed, he persuaded the Father Guardian to receive the whole party as lodgers; they were taken to the guest rooms forthwith and shown every courtesy before they lay down to sleep.

Other, more docile, pilgrims had accepted the accommodation offered them and had already gone to bed. Next morning, however, the enterprising Fra Francesco sought out "certain pilgrims of special consequence", inviting them to join the Milanese at Mount Syon. The Capodilista cousins were among these selected guests; Gabriele was pleased to note in his *Itinerario* that no extra charge was made for the new quarters: the friars accepted without comment the customary rate.[5]

When they assembled early on Sunday, June 25th, even the most impatient pilgrims learned—if they had not already discovered it from their guide-books—that they could not be admitted to the Church of the Holy Sepulchre except at stated times, as marked upon their permits. The church was open only at this one time of the year; after the last pilgrims had departed it would be locked again until the following season.† Two Franciscans, acting as 'Guardians of the Holy Sepulchre', would remain within the church, to maintain the lamps and watch over the altars. They would be fed, as was

---

* These had been established for more than a century. Normally there were twenty-four brethren, in addition to the half dozen who resided at Bethlehem. A generation later they had improved their hostel arrangements and were much more willing to accept lodgers.

† The Muslim *custos* kept the key in his own possession. The church is still locked at night.

customary, by their brethren, the food being pushed to them through a wicket or hole in the outer door. As soon as next year's pilgrims made an appearance these brethren would be released from their duties.

Itineraries had been carefully drawn up by Loredan, in consultation with the Muslim guide named Mahomet who had been seconded to their party. Some of the Holy Places accommodated several traditions, so that a single inspection could cover a number of pious exercises and indulgences might be accumulated. This was convenient for those who had come such a long way and who had so short a time: as in the church of S. Stefano in Bologna today, where tourists pressed for time can visit a variety of churches under one roof. Much depended, therefore, upon the brain-work and team-work of their leaders. Loredan seems to have possessed a gift for organization; none of his pilgrims complained that he interfered with their liberty, yet they evidently covered the ground with great thoroughness, re-visiting a second or even a third time those shrines that meant most to them. It was, indeed, a thoroughly satisfactory schedule.

Neither Sanseverino's nor Capodilista's account of the Holy Places differs materially from the descriptions given by Wey and many other writers. Their personal impressions are seldom recorded. In one single day, between sunrise and sunset, they explored the Vale of Syloe, the Vale of Josaphat, Mount Syon, and the Mount of Olives, but they were not always expected to work at their sightseeing at quite that pressure. Sometimes they wandered back to the fringes of their conducted tours to mark anew the place where the Apostles composed the Creed, or the tree on which Judas hanged himself, or to examine once again the stone in the church on the Mount of Olives, tracing the footprint said to have been imprinted there by Christ when He ascended into Heaven. The only place that really disappointed Roberto was the Garden of Gethsemane. He does not say what he expected to see, but he complains that he found it "uncultivated" and a tangle of vegetation. Capodilista also describes Gethsemane as "uncultivated at the present time, but full of olive trees"; he meditated here for a long time upon Christ's Agony, on St. Peter's impetuous attack upon Malchus, and the incredulity of St. Thomas. Finally, he recorded the prayer that he said in this place;[6] clearly this was one of the Holy Places that appealed most to him.

Capodilista occasionally departs from the catalogue-like list of 'things seen': this gives his narrative a special quality, as in his account of his visit to Pilate's house, when he turned aside to discover "on my right hand a humble little house, known as the School of Mary because it was here that the Virgin Mary used to go to learn her letters in the days of her early childhood. . . . I was very pleased to happen upon this in a blind alley that I easily might have missed."[7]

Our Lady's house, of course, was visited by every pilgrim. The house of St. Anne, mother of the Virgin, was, however, a more difficult proposition since it had been taken over by the Muslims and converted into a mosque. It was thus out of bounds for Christian visitors, but since it ranked among the Holy Places arrangements had been made whereby it could be visited discreetly. In this one instance the Muslims were ready to turn a blind eye. Some fifty years after Roberto's visit Sir Richard Guylforde's chaplain reported that it could be entered "pryuely or for brybes";[8] Loredan's arrangements must have been good, for the pilgrims in 1458 seem to have gone there as a matter of course, without any trouble at all. Other buildings with Christian associations that had been turned into mosques were jealously guarded from intrusion. Pilgrims had to be satisfied, as Roberto said, "with an external view". Few were as foolhardy as the Spaniard Pero Tafur, who disguised himself as a Muslim in order to venture into the Mosque of Omar, courting certain death should his identity be discovered. Tafur boasted about his adventure in his *Travels*,[9] but his

action was neither praised nor emulated by more conventional pilgrims, however tourist-minded they might be.

It was natural enough that pilgrims should notice a
resemblance between the monuments they were visiting
and familiar institutions in their own home towns—the
church perhaps where they customarily worshipped or had
themselves been baptized. The Church of the Holy
Sepulchre, for instance, reminded Canon Pietro Casola of
S. Lorenzo at Milan,[10] but to Capodilista it spoke of his
beloved S. Antonio in Padua.[11] He compared it also to S.
Francesco, Bologna, just as the relics he was shown in
Palestine recalled to his mind those he had seen eighteen
years earlier at Notre Dame in Paris, perhaps in his student
days.[12] There are few personal allusions in Roberto's
narrative at this point; he is content to give an account of
his itinerary that could well have been copied from Capodilista's with most of the devotions omitted. Where Gabriele
fills out his description with the private prayers that he
considers appropriate, Sanseverino makes accurate notes of
times and distances, reserving his own commentary for
the later stages of his pilgrimage. In this, as in other ways,
the diarists are complementary to one another; ostensibly
they share the same experiences, but in reality they lived
in different worlds appropriate to their individual qualities
of emotion, character and mind.

THE HOLY SEPULCHRE

On Tuesday, 27th June . . . they visited the Church
of the Holy Sepulchre for the second time . . . and
the said Earl [of Worcester] after he had knighted
them with a golden sword . . . reminded them how
great was the honour of receiving this dedication
in so precious and holy a place.

Roberto da Sanseverino:
Viaggio in Terra Santa, 1458

Their first visit to the Church of the Holy Sepulchre was
to many of the pilgrims the climax of their religious life.
It was certainly the highest peak of their sightseeing tour of
Jerusalem. The Brothers of Mount Syon had instructed
and admonished the whole party so thoroughly that there
could be no excuse for either ignorance or ill-behaviour.
The pilgrims rose on that Sunday, June 25th, an hour before
sunrise in their anxiety to be ready for the promised expedition; they had to wait with what patience they could until
the two brethren were ready to lead them to the 'piazza'
whence they would be admitted to the church in an orderly
manner, two by two, under the Muslim doorkeeper's
scrutiny. The entrance fee, amounting to only a few pence,
had already been paid by the *patrono*, Antonio Loredan, in
accordance with his undertaking.

The nervous strain was too great for some of the party;
while certain pilgrims wept tempestuously, others felt sick
or faint. It was considered becoming to demonstrate one's
feelings freely; a German Dominican was deeply shocked
by those "brute beasts" and "dull unprofitable souls" who

showed no emotion on this great occasion; he himself was profoundly moved, in sympathy with those of his companions who gave vent to their feelings with "groans, sweet wailings, and deep sighs."[1] On the other hand, such exhibitionism could be overdone. An Englishwoman of an earlier generation continually embarrassed her companions by her extravagant religious fervour "even at meals"; as she approached the Holy Sepulchre she "cried and made wondrous faces and expressions" to such an extent that the rest of her party, from shame at her lack of control, passed to fury as they vainly tried to restrain her "boisterous weeping".[2]

While they were waiting for admission to the church, the pilgrims sat about in the courtyard. The more conventionally religious were occupied with their devotions; others silently contemplated the exterior of the church, speculating about its dimensions and noting such details as the little wicket-gate in the wall through which the custodians were fed by their brethren. Others again amused themselves with conversation or restored their tissues with figs and wine, or even played cards or chess as they sat on the benches provided for their comfort. They can be seen doing all these things in the picture* drawn for Antonio Capodilista's manuscript of the *Itinerario*.[3] Many pilgrims have left descriptions, some factual, others romantic, of their experiences as they waited for admission to the holy place they had come so far to see: nowhere else are they actually represented in so natural a manner. The gold and delicate colours of this miniature are as fresh today as they ever were: as fresh as the spirit of inquiry and innocent devotion that led this party of pilgrims over these much-trodden ways.

Not only pilgrims thronged the courtyard. The picture shows Muslim officials, sitting cross-legged upon the marble benches as they waited to examine and to stamp the

* See plates.

pilgrims' permits to enter, or to question Loredan and the Franciscan brothers about their credentials. There were water sellers too, and hucksters of fruit and eggs and crisp white loaves. As the sun rose towards its meridian those who could not bear its rays moved into the shade, while the shadows grew shorter and the blistering heat increased. There was constant movement and fidgeting. By the time admission was allowed, the pilgrims—although they passed through the cordon of officials meekly in pairs as they had been directed—once they were inside the church went surging into the gloom of the interior forgetful of all the instruction they had so recently been given. In their excitement they chattered to one another, their voices magnified and echoing from the vaulted roof, mingling with importunate cries from the traders who had followed them in and were now trying to sell them candles.

As at Jaffa, when they had rushed the gangways in their anxiety to be the first to disembark, the ultramontanes tended to be the most aggressive. Perhaps they had to be of tougher fibre in order to contend with the harshness and rigours of their journeying from distant lands; perhaps it was innate prejudice that made educated Italians disdain their pushing manner. The aristocratic Canon Pietro Casola wrote "I always let the ultramontanes rush in front"; when he paid his visit to the Holy Sepulchre he waited until the crowd had passed by, then, carrying his lighted candle, he touched the shrines and relics with his rosaries "without any impediment".[4]

Those who had expected a deep hush broken only by the muted prayers of devout pilgrims were rudely astonished by the din and hubbub that filled the air in this most holy of the Holy Places. All was confusion, high-pitched conversation in many languages, the loud chaffering of traders intent upon their harvest of Venetian groats and ducats in exchange for candles, souvenirs, and relics of most improbable authenticity. One of the chief reasons for all this confusion was the number and variety of venerable sites within the church, the complex of biblical associations, the chapels to be visited, the offerings to be made, and the prayers to be recited. At last the pilgrims suffered themselves to be organized into an orderly procession. Then, each holding his candle and chanting the prescribed hymns, they moved from place to place. Eighteen steps led to the chapel of Mount Calvary; here the pilgrims inspected the hole in which the Cross of Christ was fixed, meditated with tears and prayers upon the Crucifixion, and were shown the spot where "it is said, the head of Adam was found".[5]

Besides the actual chapel of the Sepulchre, that surprised many of the pilgrims by its small size—"only nine palms in length",* wrote an Irish pilgrim who seems to have been an accurate observer[6]—there were many other shrines. There was the beautiful subterranean church where St. Helena, mother of the Emperor Constantine, found the wood of the Cross; "the place where Nicodemus and Joseph of Arimathea washed the Body of Jesus," the place where He appeared to Mary Magdalen, "the spot where the Blessed Virgin Mary grieved for her Son hanging upon the Cross".[7] Roberto noted the chapel of St. Mary of Egypt; "for the sake of brevity and clearness"[8] he summarized his list according to the indulgences obtainable "at every sacred shrine", leaving his more detailed observations to be recorded during his second visit. There were chapels maintained by Nestorians, Copts, Armenians and other Christians regarded as schismatics; Roberto was surprised to find that Muslims also regarded this as a holy place: "Not only Christians, but Saracens as well, visit the Church of the Holy Sepulchre with the greatest reverence, even paying two *soldi* as their entrance fee."[9]

All pilgrims in Holy Orders were anxious to celebrate Mass at one of the many altars in the church; this was arranged for them by the guardians and they were allotted

* That is, about six feet. The *palmus* was reckoned to be eight to ten inches.

times and places for this pious exercise. Before he left England Tiptoft had taken care to provide himself with papal permission for his chaplains to say Mass as and when he wished. An *indult* was issued to him declaring that: "In whatsoever places he may reside, stay or lodge, he may cause masses and other divine offices to be celebrated or sung, in presence of himself and of his household, by fit priests of his choice at any fit or suitable hour, and that such priests may, as often as it shall be expedient, and it shall seem good to him and them, administer to him and his said household the sacrament of Eucharist and other sacraments."[10] Thus, Tiptoft and his chaplains and the whole body of pilgrims were able to practise their devotions without dependence upon the brethren of Mount Syon. Tiptoft had also applied for permission for one of his chaplains to say Mass "on Mount Calvary"; this was duly granted. The chaplain chosen for this privilege was probably John Hurlegh who had been in the Earl's household since they were fellow students at Oxford,[11] and who crowned this long friendship by bequeathing to Tiptoft "a covered cup of silver-gilt weighing eighteen ounces"[12] just two years before Tiptoft's own death.

The sermon was preached by "an English priest, a Fellow of Eton"; this must have been William Wey himself for he recorded the fact in his *Itineraries*, mentioning that the theme of the discourse was "Peregrinus es in Jerusalem".

Two days later the pilgrims paid their second visit to the church. "But because the pilgrims were many and the space round the Holy Sepulchre very limited, their visit . . . was deferred until after nightfall." This time they planned to pass the whole night there, with a minimum of sleep and long hours of prayer and meditation. Since most of the pilgrims had spent all day in strenuous sightseeing, when evening came they were both tired and hungry. Their first thought was to collect provisions to sustain them during their vigil, picnic fare of fruit and hard-boiled eggs and goats-milk cheese. After revisiting the chapels and repeating the proper devotions, nearly all the pilgrims composed themselves for sleep, locked into the building as they were, secure from all distraction. "The whole visitation completed and the aforesaid places inspected again," wrote Roberto,[13] "they lay down to sleep so that they would be able to rise in the morning to hear Mass, according to the praiseworthy custom of pilgrims. They slept, moreover, in the church lying on choristers' surplices, or mats, or upon the bare floor, each according to his choice."

When the great doors of the church were opened next morning, as soon as Mass was over, the pilgrims came out into the strong daylight, standing in the courtyard for a few moments to collect their wits and to decide what their next move should be. Loredan was there, discussing with the Guardian and the Muslim officials the best means of escorting the main body of the pilgrims to Bethlehem. As this expedition was included in their contract the pilgrims did not have to pay any further dues; they were content to leave all the arrangements to Loredan, who completed his plans rapidly and without fuss.

One more ceremony remained to be carried out in the Church of the Holy Sepulchre. While Carlo Bosso and the others were visiting Bethlehem, Roberto da Sanseverino and Butigella persuaded the Guardian to allow one of the party to confer knighthood upon two Milanese who sought the honour. These were Butigella himself and the absent Bosso. The military Order of the Knights of the Holy Sepulchre was a chivalrous institution at this time presided over by the King of Aragon;* the Father Guardian of Mount Syon had authority to admit to the Order pilgrims who were eligible for this honour through their nobility of birth and military distinction. As a rule knighthood was conferred by one of the brethren who was himself a noble: this was a

* Alfonso V. He died June 27th, 1458 but, of course, the news had not yet reached Jerusalem.

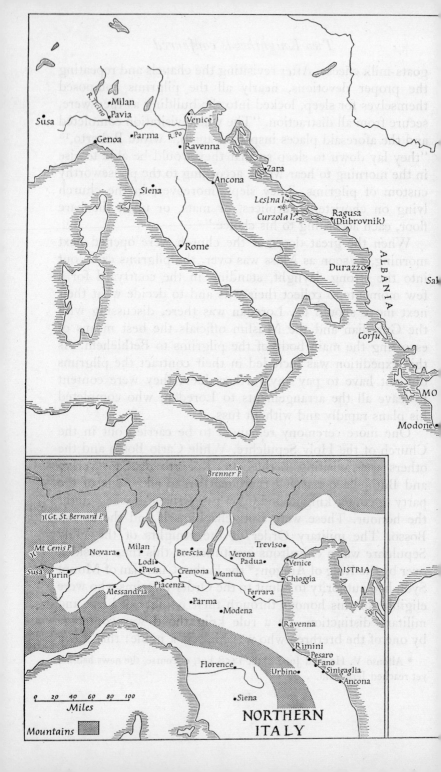

Labels on the map (upper, Italy and Adriatic):

Susa • Milan • Pavia • R. Ticino • Venice • Genoa • Parma • R. Po • Ravenna • Zara • Ancona • Siena • Lesina I. • Curzola I. • Ragusa (Dubrovnik) • Rome • Durazzo • ALBANIA • Corfu • Modone

Labels on the map (lower, detail):

Brenner P. •)(Gt. St. Bernard P. • Mt Cenis P. • Novara • Milan • Brescia • Treviso • Verona • Padua • Venice • Susa • Turin • Lodi • Pavia • Cremona • Mantua • Chioggia • ISTRIA • Alessandria • Piacenza • Ferrara • Parma • Modena • Ravenna • Rimini • Pesaro • Florence • Urbino • Fano • Sinigaglia • Ancona • Siena

0 20 40 60 80 100
Miles

Mountains

NORTHERN ITALY

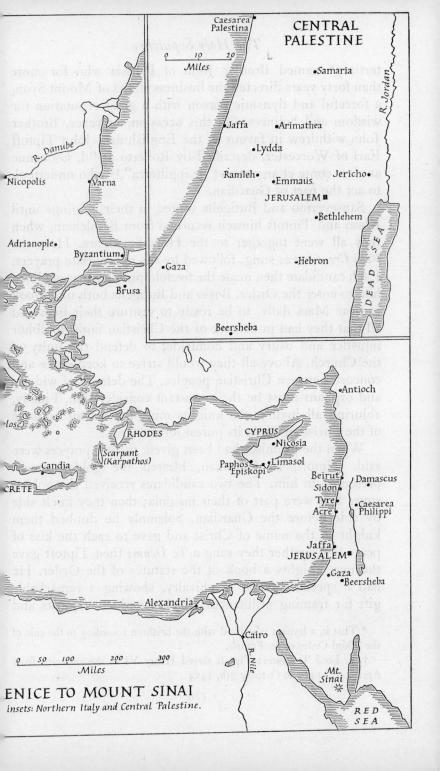

CENTRAL PALESTINE

VENICE TO MOUNT SINAI

insets: Northern Italy and Central Palestine.

tertiary* named Brother John of Prussia who for more than forty years directed the business affairs of Mount Syon, a forceful and dynamic person with a great reputation for wisdom and holiness. On this occasion, however, Brother John withdrew in favour of the Englishman, John Tiptoft Earl of Worcester, described by Roberto as "d. Giouanne anglese conte et argentero† de ingilterra",[14] who undertook to act the part of Guardian.

Sanseverino and Butigella waited in their lodgings until Bosso and Tiptoft himself returned from Bethlehem, when they all went together to the Holy Sepulchre. Here the *Veni Creator* was sung, followed by the appropriate prayers. Each candidate then made the fivefold promise that qualified him to enter the Order. Bosso and Butigella both undertook to hear Mass daily, to be ready to venture their lives and all that they had in defence of the Christian faith, to abhor injustice and usury and homicide, to defend the unity of the Church. Above all they would strive to keep peace and concord between Christian peoples. The defence of widows and orphans must be their constant consideration. Finally, abjuring all luxury, the knights must present an example of the Christian life in its purest form.

When the promises had been given, further prayers were said. Tiptoft, as Guardian, blessed the golden sword presented to him. The two candidates received the golden spurs that were part of their insignia; then they knelt side by side before the Guardian. Solemnly he dubbed them knight in the name of Christ and gave to each the kiss of peace.[15] Together they sang a *Te Deum*; then Tiptoft gave the new knights a book of the statutes of the Order. He had a special interest in chivalry, showing a remarkable gift for framing ordinances for the conduct of jousts and

---

* That is, a layman who lived with the brethren according to the rule of the Third Order of St. Francis.

† i.e. Lord Treasurer: Tiptoft served Henry VI in this capacity from April 15th, 1452 to October 7th, 1454.

A Memorable Ceremony concluded

tourneys and laying down procedure at state functions of
every kind. Indeed, since Tiptoft was such a notable
authority on these matters[16] it was fitting and appropriate
that he should conduct the ceremony. He was, moreover,
an excellent orator: the homily that he delivered to the new
knights and the assembled company was a model of its
kind. Sanseverino was so impressed by the speech that he
recorded a summary of it in his *Viaggio*. At last the pageantry
came to an end. In sober mood they all departed from the
church, Bosso and Butigella mindful of their vows, and the
whole party deeply conscious of the fact pointed out to them
by Tiptoft that the profession had been made in a uniquely
precious and holy place.[17] It was the most dramatic of all
their experiences in the Church of the Holy Sepulchre
and the one that would stay longest in their minds.

9

BETHLEHEM

From Jerusalem to Bethleem ben fyue myles and
is the hyghe waye . . . is the place where the sterre
apperyd to ye Kynges of Coleyne. . . . In Bethleem
is a fayre chirche of our lady in whȳche is a place
where Crist was born. . . . Also two myles on the
north syde from Bethleem is an olde broken chyrche
where the angell aperyd to the shepeherdes.

Information for Pilgrims unto the Holy Land

It had been the original intention of Carlo Bosso and his
two friends who had joined the Milanese party in Pavia,
to accompany Roberto on his expedition to Mount Sinai
"and other places not normally visited by pilgrims". At
some point of his pilgrimage, however, he had experienced
a change of heart, deciding to forego the extension of the
tour. Although the Holy Mountain was so rewarding in its
associations with history and religion, although many
indulgences could be gained by visiting its shrines, the fact
remained that the Monastery of St. Catherine was set in
such remote and mountainous country that the journey
there was formidable indeed. Moreover, Sanseverino
believed that Bosso—who had suffered very severely from
sea-sickness on the outward journey—dared not risk the
storms that must be expected during an autumn voyage.[1]
Bosso thought that it might be wiser to leave the Holy
Land not later than the beginning of July and there was
much to be said for his point of view. He, together with
Fenone de Eustachio, Domenico da Lodi, and Butigella's
servant Hilario Gentili of Tortona, resolved to return home

with the rest of the pilgrims in Loredan's party. Their final sightseeing, therefore, had to be crammed into the few days remaining to them before they must turn their faces westwards towards Jaffa.

Sanseverino and Butigella could afford to take things more easily, since they would have further opportunities for visiting the Holy Places outside Jerusalem and for making journeys to Bethlehem and the Jordan Valley. They stayed quietly at Mount Syon, writing letters for Bosso to carry back to Milan,* while the other pilgrims spent the night at Bethlehem. This was the evening of Monday, June 26th. It so happens that the letter Butigella wrote that day to Francesco Sforza has survived;[2] Roberto's, unfortunately, is missing.

While the letter writers were at work, Carlo Bosso, the Capodilista cousins, John Tiptoft, and some forty others of the party set out for Bethlehem. To avoid the heat of the day they did not start until evening. The road was a pleasant one to travel, the going was easy, all were in the best of spirits. Vines, figs, and olives grew by the roadside, there were gardens and wells of ice-cold water: one pilgrim found this road from Jerusalem to Bethlehem "the most beautiful" he had seen "in all those parts".[3] It was nearly night-time when they reached the outskirts of the little town, too dark to see clearly the ruinous condition of the place or to notice how scarred and mouldering were the beams supporting the roof of what had been a noble church built above the cave where the Holy Child was born.

The forty-four pilgrims were deeply moved by this their first visit to the Cave of Bethlehem. As they took their candles and descended to the grotto they felt awe and wonder, and a devotion even more overwhelming than at

---

* Butigella's letter is endorsed: "written from the Monastery of Mount Syon in the holy city of Jerusalem"; it is little more than an ordinary exercise in civility. He wrote a small elegant hand, more sophisticated than the rough bold handwriting of Sanseverino.

their first view of the Holy Sepulchre. This was in some ways the crowning experience of their whole pilgrimage. The peace and quietness of the place was in strong contrast to the distracting noises that were ever present in Jerusalem. It was for all of them a great and solemn moment.

That night the pilgrims stayed with the six Franciscan brothers. These had a convent where they were accustomed to house guests; the friars here were subsidiary to the brothers of Mount Syon, who notified them in advance when a party of pilgrims was about to arrive. Next morning everyone attended a choral Mass sung by Tiptoft's chaplains at the altar of Christ's Nativity.[4] Afterwards they examined the beauties and treasures of the church. In the strong sunlight they were able to see the mosaics glittering with gold that decorated the entrance to the birthplace, and to mark the "extraordinary whiteness" of the marble manger. Some hours were spent in studying these and all the sites connected with the life of Christ—the well whence the Magi drew water and another into which had fallen the star that guided them, the cave where the bodies of the Holy Innocents had been thrown, and many more.

It was late afternoon before the pilgrims were free to seek the hillside where the shepherds watched their flocks before the angel announced to them the birth of Jesus. In the valley stood a ruined church commemorating the place where the shepherds heard the angels sing *Gloria in Excelsis*; the holy mount was more difficult to find. Gabriele Capodilista, John Tiptoft, and several others made inquiries from the friars; they were told that the *monticulo* was just a mile from the centre of Bethlehem and could be easily identified. It turned out to be a hillock set in a valley surrounded by other low hills. As they prepared to make their devotions, one pilgrim, who had visited Palestine before, told them "in a loud voice" that they were in the wrong place, claiming that the true holy mount was another of the little hills. A great argument developed: Gabriele called it "devota alterchatione";[5] he strenuously defended his own point of view. While the pilgrims wrangled, he tells us, the matter was settled by divine intervention. A "shooting star" or meteorite fell upon the *monticulo* where they sat or stood, thus demonstrating "beyond all doubt" that they were in the right place. All the pilgrims fell upon their knees to give thanks "to God for His clemency"; they then resumed their pious explorations with renewed enthusiasm.

Gabriele Capodilista was too civilized a person to glory in his opponent's defeat. He was pleased, of course, to have been proved right, but he showed his customary magnanimity in giving the contentious pilgrim credit for his honest doubt. This was perhaps a foretaste of the charity carried almost to a caricature that Gabriele showed when he afterwards became Podestà of Perugia.[6] Here, when a German friar, Brother Vinterio, stole for his own convent Our Lady's Wedding Ring from the cathedral at Chiusi and was arraigned before him, Capodilista found that although the case was proved, Brother Vinterio should be pardoned— it was the Devil's fault for tempting him too highly. After all, he said, other "holy thieves" had been rewarded by beatification.

There were many other interesting places in and about Bethlehem for the pilgrims to visit, from the well of David just outside the gate to the sepulchre of St. Jerome and the place where, as Master Larkes* said, "he torned the Byble owte of Ebrewe into Latin". This was another of the limestone caves that honeycombed the landscape hereabouts, flanked by olive-groves and guarded by slender cypress trees standing upright like dark sentinels. The ground fell away from the walls of the little town in a gentle slope where flocks still grazed as in the time of Christ, and the field of Boaz where Ruth had gleaned still carried its crop of corn.

* If we accept him, as I think we may, as the author of the *Information for Pilgrims*. See above, p. 19.

The hours passed all too quickly; as dusk fell the pilgrims paid a last visit to the Church of the Nativity, then mounted their donkeys for the ride back to Jerusalem.

Next day, all the pilgrims except the three Milanese—who planned to make the expedition later on—went to bathe in the River Jordan. To plunge into these muddy but sacred waters was a great experience, one that no pilgrim would willingly forgo. The bathers believed that they were renewing their youth as well as expressing their devotion to their faith. Foolhardy pilgrims who dived headlong into the lukewarm stream were sometimes drowned, for the bottom was soft and the water turbid; in the excitement they might easily stick in the mud or be trampled underfoot by the crowd of bathers. Many brought belts or strips of material to dip in the precious water; some even smuggled it away in phials. This had to be done very secretly, for sailors believed that Jordan water caused storms when it was carried over the sea. They were likely to treat very roughly any pilgrims caught in possession of such relics. It was safer, as well as more convenient, to gather a handful of coloured pebbles to carry home as souvenirs.

The excursion to the Jordan was on this occasion extended to include Mount Quarantana where Christ fasted forty days and nights. On the Feast of SS. Peter and Paul, June 29th, the pilgrims stumbled on through the craggy barren waste to the hillside, desolate and windswept, of the Mount of Temptation (as it was called by later generations). The road curved and twisted round great outcrops of dull grey stone; the loose surface made the way slow and difficult: this was quite the worst going that the pilgrims had experienced. Their donkeys liked it as little as they did; all were hot, bored and thirsty. William Wey, as always, had helpful advice to offer. "Hyt ys passyng hote and ryght hye", he wrote in his *Itineraries*, "when ye come downe a yen for nothyng drynke no water, but rest yow a lytyl, and then ette brede and drynke clene wyne w\u1d57owte water; after that grete hete water generyth a gret fluxe, other a fever, other bothe, than a man may haply lose hys lyfe thereby." Wey warned his readers venturing on such expeditions that they must not rely on finding food by the way, but should pack provisions for at least two days—hard cheese, bread, hard-boiled eggs, and the good red wine that could be bought—at a price—in Jerusalem.

The descent from the mountain was nearly as difficult as the upward struggle and perhaps more dangerous because of the quantity of loose scree. As the pilgrims returned from this, the last of their exploratory journeys, they had a strong feeling of accomplishment, but there can be little doubt that most of them carried home as their most impressive memory the silence and darkness of the crib at Bethlehem.

It was not for nothing that Sanseverino and Butigella made this village their centre for leisurely explorations of the countryside when the rest of the party had gone home. From this point they visited the birthplace of St. John the Baptist, the spot where an angel appeared to Our Lady on flight to Egypt in order to direct her steps along the right road, the site of David's battle with Goliath, and the church dedicated to St. George, where they were shown the chain that bound him prisoner. All these distances Roberto measured from Bethlehem; it was from here, too, that he set out upon his desert journey, and it was here that Butigella came to meet him on his return. Jerusalem might be the centre of the Christian's world, but the pilgrims' chief preoccupation was with the little town of Bethlehem.

THE SHORT WAY HOME

On their way home from Jerusalem Messer Antonio
and Messer Gabriele landed [on the island of
Cyprus]. Mounting horses they rode all through
the night . . . to visit Messer Andrea Cornaro, by
whom they were received with exquisite courtesy.
                              Gabriele Capodilista:
                         Itinerario in Terra Santa, 1458

As the time allotted for their tour ran out, the pilgrims
finished packing their belongings and the souvenirs they
had collected. In a scramble of last-minute shopping they
bought small presents to take home to their friends, with
further relics to remind them of the joys and benefits they
had personally experienced. Not for these pilgrims exotic
merchandise, jewels, carpets, or expensive silks and perfumes. They were content with models of the Holy
Sepulchre, the church at Bethlehem, and the chapel on
Mount Calvary, all carved out of olive-wood, or represen-
tations painted on cloth of the Mount of Olives and the
Temple at Jerusalem. They might buy curtains of blue
buckram but never of cloth of gold. Neither the Paduans
nor John Tiptoft were the sort of 'milords' to waste money
on extravagant souvenirs; the rest of the party may have
desired to do so but lacked the means. A generation earlier
Henry Earl of Derby had brought home from his pilgrimage
an ostrich and a leopard (that needed "much attention and
care"):[1] there is no evidence that any of the pilgrims in
1458 bought himself so much as a popinjay.

By the end of June the pilgrims were ready to leave.

Antonio Loredan summoned all those who were to return
to Venice in the two galleys, preparing to lead them back
to Jaffa. Only Sanseverino, Butigella, and Giovanni Martino,
together with their servants, stayed on with the Brothers
of Mount Syon; everyone else had decided against the
expedition to Mount Sinai. On June 30th William Wey
left Jerusalem with the first contingent; by July 2nd they
were safely at Jaffa. They went aboard their old ship
immediately, putting out to sea that very night. Three
days later the *Loredana* sailed with Bosso's party, Tiptoft
and the rest. As soon as Loredan had handed over his
charges to Baldessare Diedo, after seeing them safely
aboard and making sure that everyone was in possession of
the gear he had left in the captain's care, he abandoned
the party in order to travel inland to see to his own affairs.
Throughout this voyage Diedo's authority was absolute.

At first all went splendidly on board the *Loredana*. The
passengers discovered stores of cushions, rugs, and bedding
that had been left in the galley by Roberto's party; these
they borrowed for their sleeping quarters and for reclining
upon deck. Everyone knew it was likely to be a laborious
voyage, for even if the ship avoided storms they would have
to head into contrary winds and beat their way slowly up
the Adriatic. With this in mind Diedo put in first to Cyprus
and then to Rhodes in order to buy fresh food and to refill
the water-barrels, but he could not allow the galley to remain
in port for more than a day or two lest the *Loredana* should
be caught by equinoctial gales before she could reach the
safety of the lagoon. Diedo's precautions were well justified
for, although they passed by several ports where they had
dropped anchor on the outward run, the voyage took seven
weeks and a day against the five weeks from Venice to
Jaffa.

When they were told that the *Loredana* would touch at
Cyprus, Gabriele and Antonio Capodilista drew up a plan
to make the most of a brief holiday. As soon as they could

jump ashore they hurried off to hire horses—late in the evening as it was. All night they rode across the island by moonlight, over perilous ways. When dawn came they found that they were still some distance from Nicosia, but by mid-day they reached this city where they met their old friend Andrea Cornaro. As before, he showed them great friendliness and courtesy; moreover he arranged for the Paduans to visit King John II, just then staying at the friars' convent. The King seemed to Gabriele to be in good health and spirits; nevertheless he died only three weeks later,[2] worn out, it was said, by his own debauchery. John II was neither a good man nor a wise ruler; according to a Spanish traveller who was present at his coronation, his chief claim to distinction was the extraordinary shape and girth of his legs which were said to be perfectly cylindrical.[3]

At this time Cyprus was a bone of contention between Venice and Genoa; since the ruling house favoured the Venetian connection the Capodilista cousins, being (as Paduans) Venetian subjects, were welcome guests. The King showed Gabriele much honour, "greeting him as a brother".[4] The same night the cousins returned with Cornaro to his house, where they rested after their long ride. They spent the next day with their host, exploring the terrain and admiring "the profusion of citrus and other delicious fruits" in his groves and gardens. At nightfall they returned to the *Loredana*. As soon as all were aboard Diedo weighed anchor; within an hour they were again at sea.

For the second visit to Rhodes it is necessary to turn to the pages of William Wey's *Itineraries*: Gabriele has nothing further to say about the island, possibly he and Antonio did not trouble to land there when the *Loredana* called. Wey tells us that he and his friends gladly went ashore, to stretch their legs and to enjoy a change of diet. It was here that the pilgrims heard the news of the day. They had been out of touch with events for so many weeks that any item of home news or gossip brought to the island by passing vessels seemed interesting and important. As usual, the people of Rhodes were pre-occupied by their savagely hostile relations with their Turkish enemies. Eighteen Christian boys had just been captured by the Turks; the Rhodians described to the pilgrims their probable fate, dwelling upon the tortures and bizarre methods of death that the Turks employed. The Knights themselves were hardly blameless; only a few weeks earlier they had seized two hundred and fifty Turks whom they had murdered with bestial savagery. Some victims were hanged, other impaled while still living, the rest hewn into small pieces. Tales of this massacre were circulated through the island with glee, but it is said that when the Sultan Mahomet II, the fierce conqueror of Constantinople,[5] heard of the practices of the Christian Knights, he turned pale. John Tiptoft Earl of Worcester—'The Butcher of England'—perhaps took his idea of mutilating and impaling the bodies of his victims from this example at Rhodes, although his savageries were inflicted only after death.[6]

The remainder of the voyage seems to have been uneventful. The *Loredana* reached Venice without mishap on September 6th; the pilgrims scrambled ashore with jubilation, their great adventure completed. As long as their money lasted, pilgrims were seldom in a hurry to reach home, especially the ultramontanes who had now to face the great barrier of the Alps. Sometimes they lingered in Venice for several days or weeks in order to recover health and spirits after the privations of their voyage. A young Milanese nobleman who returned from Palestine a few years later than Diedo's passengers was so "overwhelmed by sea-sickness" that it was twelve days before he could mount his horse for the last stage of his journey.[7]

There was no need for Gabriele and Antonio to delay their return to Padua, only a few hours distant from their landing stage. As soon as they had given thanks for their

safe return the cousins set out for home, where they received
—as they had expected—the warmest of welcomes from
their friends and kindred. It is to be supposed that Gabriele's
Itinerario was circulated from hand to hand; immediately
upon arrival Antonio put in hand the writing of a very
sumptuous copy that he intended to give to the Abbess of
the Convent of S. Bernardino in Padua.[8] Gabriele wrote her
a special dedicatory letter, explaining that he had marked
in the margin "with a red cross" all minor indulgences that
could be obtained in the Holy Places, and with a golden
one all that carried a plenary indulgence. The original
draft of the *Itinerario* was, of course, much simpler, for it
was jotted down from day to day as the journey progressed,
without the adventitious aids of red ink and gold leaf.[9]

Gabriele Capodilista's friendship with the Earl of
Worcester was not broken, for the Englishman accompanied
him to Padua and began to study in the University. As a
youth he had read law at Oxford but had been obliged to
break off his studies before taking his degree when his
father, the first Earl, died. As explained in Chapter 2,
John Tiptoft had to forego the life among books and scholars
that he found so congenial, in order to manage his family
estates and to begin an unhappy association with politics
that led to his execution in 1470. The three years he spent
in Italy, attending lectures, buying handsome manuscripts,
and associating with urbane and intelligent people, were the
best and most profitable of his life. It was not until he was
peremptorily summoned home by King Edward IV[10] that
Tiptoft could be persuaded to leave his studies in order to
submerge himself in the futile activities of the military
caste into which he had been born.

The rest of the Englishmen, all the Germans, and others
who had come from northern lands, made their way home
by the Brenner, the easiest of all the passes. Some had to
beg their way for the last few hundred miles; all were tired
and travelworn by their experiences. It took Wey seven

weeks to return from Venice to Dover, whereas this journey could be made at speed in twenty-five days. Indeed, the average time taken for letter post between London and Venice was agreed to be just under four weeks.[11] Little is known of this band of pilgrims after they reached home; there are few personal notes in their descriptions of their travels. Even Wey, the most lively of them, although his narrative is self-revealing up to a point, gives no indication of what befell him in later life. We know from other sources that he vacated his Fellowship at Eton about the year 1467, dying nine years later at Edington in Wiltshire where he had become an Austin canon. His possessions of books, plate, and altar-cloths were divided between his old college at Oxford (Exeter) and King Henry's new foundation at Eton, but the fruits of his pilgrimage, the relics and the "stones", Wey left to Edington along with his mortal remains.

D. Antonio Lauredano and other Venetian merchants were then in Damascus . . . Roberto asked
him to send . . . certain delicacies, sugar, comfits
and other such things, so that he [Roberto] would
have them for the homeward voyage.

Roberto da Sanseverino:
Viaggio in Terra Santa, 1458[1]

Like the true Venetian he was, Loredan's word was as
good as his bond, but no better. As soon as he had handed
over the pilgrims to Diedo's care he switched his attention
to the business of making money under cover of his position
as pilgrims' protector and guide. Loredan had been in this
profession for eighteen years, he came from an ancient
patrician family that had a long record of service in the
transport of pilgrims; he was also by tradition and upbring-
ing a keen business man.

Antonio Loredan, like his father before him, had applied
for the captaincy of a galley at an early age, for the ordinance
that no licensed captain should be under thirty had not yet
been enacted. Together with his cousin Lorenzo and an
older, more experienced captain, the young Antonio had
been successful in the auction of licences for the autumn
voyage in 1440.[2] That year it happened that there were
in the party under his care some foreign pilgrims "of notable
condition". These applied to the Senate for special permission "to carry certain merchandise", since there were few
of them on board and there would therefore be plenty of
room for cargo. As a general rule the Venetian Senate was

strongly opposed to the carrying of passengers' goods other than their personal luggage. They believed that this practice might lead to abuses of several kinds; above all there was danger that valuable merchandise might be smuggled into Venetian territory under the noses of customs officers who would be looking only for the souvenirs ordinarily imported by pilgrims. On the other hand, the Senate liked to accede to the whims of important foreign visitors, when these did not seem to interfere with serious business. On May 11th, 1440, then, a special licence was granted, although the Senate did not agree to its issue without prolonged argument.[3]

This concession began a profitable side-line for Antonio. Although the Senate continued to discourage attempts at trading with Palestine by either passengers or crew of the pilgrim galleys, Loredan now had his contacts and quickly developed his system. Of course the *galeotti* traded quite openly in the ports where the galleys touched, but since their business was with the passengers they had little occasion to evade the customs dues. This practice, therefore, was allowed. Indeed, it could hardly have been stopped, so traditional had it become. The Senate, as always, took a realistic view of the situation in accepting what could not be prevented.

On July 3rd, 1458, having seen his charges safely on board, Loredan left Jaffa for Damascus. Here he planned to buy the fine Eastern silks that were his speciality; he allowed himself several weeks for this purpose, for no one knew better that bargaining with Oriental traders to be successful must also be extremely protracted. Loredan made Damascus his base of operations because it was the most important trading centre in Syria, second only to Alexandria in the spice trade and surpassing even that great market in the high quality of silks and precious stones brought on camel-back from Persia and distant parts of Asia.

There were in Damascus—as in several other Syrian

cities—small pockets of Christian traders. Besides Loredan
and the Venetian friends associated with him in his enter-
prises,[4] there were various other Italian merchants, mostly
from Genoa or Ancona. There were Frenchmen, too,
notably the agents of the famous Jacques Cœur of Bourges
who concentrated on buying great quantities of spices to be
shipped directly from Beirut to Narbonne. All the Christians
were compelled to conform to strict regulations concerning
hours of trading. Indeed, they were locked into their
quarters at sundown and were not allowed to open their
warehouses until after dawn the next morning. Europeans
were usually wise enough to keep strictly to their own
business; as long as they were not foolishly aggressive they
could trade freely with men of other races. Occasionally
there might be a flare-up of national feeling, but it seldom
had serious consequences. One French traveller excited
derision by wearing an enormous black beaver hat as he
walked about the streets of Damascus; in a scuffle the hat
was knocked off his head and thrown to the ground. His
dignity disturbed, he shook his fist in the faces of his
tormentors, but in the end good humour prevailed and no
harm was done. "I mention this", he wrote, "to show that
the inhabitants of Damascus are a wicked race, and con-
sequently care should be taken to avoid any quarrels with
them."[5]

Buying and selling was on so massive a scale that the
Venetian Republic found it necessary to station consuls
at Damascus and Aleppo, as well as at the port of Beirut,
to protect the interests of her merchants.[6] Loredan and his
friends were constantly in touch with these officials who
were able to help them considerably. Trade with the Orient
was the life-blood of the Venetian Republic; it was only the
combination of pilgrim traffic and the freight of merchandise
that was forbidden. There was no rule against forming a
convoy of both types of galley to sail in company for safety's
sake; indeed, it was a plan that seemed both prudent and

economical, two qualities that appealed very strongly to the Venetian Senate. Antonio Loredan saw in this system a good opportunity for concealing one set of activities under the cloak of another. If he were to charter a small galley at Beirut, nominally to carry the Milanese pilgrims back to Venice, he could also take on board bales of Eastern silks stripped of their wrappings and packed in canvas so that they would appear to be the pilgrims' personal luggage. A vessel named the *Leza* lay in harbour at Beirut; she was of the right size and type and her owner was offering her for hire. The other Venetian traders joined Loredan in his project, chartering the *Leza* in his name because he was the only captain holding a licence to carry pilgrims. Loredan had made it his business to keep in close touch with Sanseverino after the other pilgrims had departed. Roberto asked the Venetian to procure for him certain luxuries for the homeward voyage, such as sugar, comfits, and other "gientilezze". Since it was not likely that the catering arrangements aboard the *Leza*, in which Roberto proposed to travel home, would be as good as in a regular pilgrim galley, he showed forethought in ordering these goods from Loredan and in writing to him several times to jog his memory.

Loredan knew very well that he would not be ready to return to Venice before at least four weeks had elapsed; by that time Sanseverino and his friends should have finished their expedition to Mount Sinai, even if they extended it, as they well might, to include Cairo. As it happened, both sets of arrangements had to be altered. Roberto postponed his journey on account of the illness of Giovanni Martino, while Loredan himself found it prudent to stay on in Damascus for fully a month after he had intended to set sail, so that he did not leave until nearly the end of September. The reason for delay was the warning he received, carried by a kind of bush telegraph, that a particularly rapacious pirate was at large in the eastern Mediterranean, ready to attack any merchant galley on sight. Moreover, he was known as a very skilful navigator; there would be no hoodwinking this man with apocryphal stories of plague on board the galley (as on the outward voyage), nor any chance of manœuvring the *Leza* out of his range. His name was Alvise Beltramo; by race he was a Catalan. Beltramo's most recent exploit had been to seize a Venetian ship at sea, looting her stores, wounding the crew, and robbing all the passengers.[7] Loredan and his friends were by no means pusillanimous; it was ordinary prudence that led them to agree to travel in convoy for protection against this corsair. The only disadvantage was that it became necessary to linger in Damascus or Beirut until the last of the captains had completed his business.

As the days and weeks slipped by, Sanseverino became increasingly impatient to depart;* in the end he made his own arrangements independently, taking ship from Acre a few days before the *Leza* and the other Venetian vessels were ready to leave Beirut. Antonio Loredan then found himself in an awkward position, since he now had no pilgrims' baggage to act as cover for his canvas-wrapped silks. He and his companions decided to bluff the matter out; in due course they made their way to Venice, arriving there several weeks before the Milanese pilgrims, who had been delayed by misfortune and incompetent seamanship.

The scrutiny of the customs officers was, however, more thorough than Loredan had hoped. His not very subtle device was quickly exposed; he and his associates were brought before the Senate and charged with fraud. The ringleader of the plot was adjudged to be a patrician named Marco Superantio, who had already been arraigned on a similar charge; he was fined two hundred *libri* and barred for life from holding office or enjoying certain privileges of citizenship. When Loredan and three others were similarly accused on November 13th, 1458, the court

* See Chapter 15.

found all of them guilty. They were made to forfeit the Syrian silks they had hidden on board the *Leza*; they were also fined[8] and disgraced.

The black mark against Antonio Loredan's name meant that there was not much future for him in the Venetian merchant fleet. Nor was he likely to obtain a *patrono's* licence for another of the pilgrim galleys, at any rate until his offence was forgotten or purged by a humiliating admission of guilt. No further trace of Loredan is found in the records of the *deliberations* of the Senate, nor in the miscellaneous items relating to overseas trade.[9] It seems that he changed his career from sailor to soldier, for some years later Loredan's name appears among the mercenary captains fighting under Sanseverino's command at the battle of Figarolo.* Since the army was encamped in the unhealthy undrained marshes near the mouth of the Po, both Sanseverino and Antonio Loredan fell gravely ill. It seemed to the enemy that the end of the war was at hand, so they began to draw up surrender terms, while Sanseverino and Loredan were carried to Padua to be nursed.[10] However, Roberto's magnificent constitution triumphed; he lived (at the age of sixty-four) to fight another day. It was the younger man who died; with Loredan's passing the link forged between pilgrim and *patrono* on the Jaffa voyage was finally broken.

All this was in the future. In 1458, when Roberto was planning his return journey, his relations with Loredan were strained nearly to breaking point. As it turned out, Roberto would have done better to wait for the *Leza* than to make an ill-considered contract to sail in a smaller ship with fewer amenities and no trained *galeotti* to help her on her way. Although she started for home later the *Leza*, under Loredan's skilled direction, actually reached Venice in excellent time; she was tied up at her moorings there while her rival was still floundering in high seas off the coast of

* In May, 1482. The enemy was Ercole d'Este, Marquis of Ferrara.

Istria. Had Roberto dipped more deeply into the 'sack of patience' recommended by the guide-books there would have been no need to quarrel with Loredan and he would have reached his destination sooner, more safely, and with less expense.

DESERT JOURNEY

. . [we] crossed the lifeless desert of Egypt with
much labour and in great peril.
Travels and Adventures of Pero Tafur, 1435-9[1]

I

For some days before the main body of pilgrims left
Jerusalem on their homeward journey, Giovanni Martino
de Ferrariis had been lying ill with dysentery. It was fortunate for him that he had developed this sickness while he
was staying in the comparative comfort of a guest-room at
Mount Syon rather than in the arid desert of Sinai, where
he would certainly have died. The brethren had a collection
of drugs suited to the needs of pilgrims suffering from the
more common diseases. They were well accustomed to
dealing with patients who succumbed to dysentery; their
infirmarius held out hopes that Giovanni Martino could
be restored to health in time to accompany his friends on the
expedition to Mount Sinai, provided they were willing
to delay their start for a few weeks.

As time passed, however, Giovanni Martino's fever rose
higher; he grew weaker daily, his friends feared that he
might die. As the patient himself was medical adviser to the
party, they had no expert help, only the devotion of the
servants* and the co-operation of the brethren in nursing
the sick man. Butigella took full responsibility for looking

* Especially his own personal servitor, Antonio Calistano, who came
from the same town (Parma) as his master, and who showed him great
loyalty.

after Giovanni Martino; he urged Sanseverino to make the desert journey alone, for it became clear that—even if he recovered his health completely—Giovanni Martino would be in no condition to travel so arduously. Butigella did not care to leave his friend; moreover, he had some slight knowledge of medicine that might prove useful. His interest in medical matters may be inferred from a letter, sent him by his friend Angelo Decembrio,[2] that accompanied a tract concerning the diagnosis and cure of "la pesta", although it does not seem that he ever studied medicine seriously.

Roberto also was very unwilling to leave Giovanni Martino, for they had planned together the itinerary and talked over the project at great length, "discussing it together wherever they happened to be, whether on board the galley or on the way to Jerusalem".[3] The journey, however, could not be put off indefinitely, for the party still expected to embark with Loredan in the *Leza*, chartered at Beirut.[4] Sanseverino "for the love and affection that he bore him" wanted Butigella to accompany him to Mount Sinai, but this he could not be persuaded to do. The friends argued the matter up and down while they revisited "many times" the Holy Places in Jerusalem, Bethlehem, and elsewhere. Butigella held firm to his promise to stay with Giovanni Martino, now more or less recovered from "the fever and the bloody flux" that had distressed him, but still pitifully debilitated. Roberto decided to take with him to Mount Sinai only his personal servant Guiniforte of Piacenza, leaving the capable Giov' Antonio Drella and the German Martin to help nurse the sick man.

It was almost the end of July when Sanseverino decided that he could wait no longer before completing his preparations. The Brethren of Mount Syon, from their long experience, were able to give him useful advice concerning his stores and equipment, and to retain on his behalf the services of the Muslim guide Mahomet, aided by an

The Day of Preparation

interpreter skilled in several languages. Very wisely Roberto
decided to join forces with a Calabrian merchant named
Antonio di Franco da Cosenza, who not only helped him
select suitable provisions but undertook also to hire the
necessary camels and donkeys with their drivers; the camels
to carry the luggage-packs, the donkeys the pilgrims.

Once his mind was made up Roberto showed himself in
his usual character as a man of action, intolerant of any delay
or hindrance to his plans. In a ferment of preparations his
servants had to collect and pack the baggage as speedily
as they could. One of the first things to do was to secure a
permit to buy the local red wine. This licence had to be
obtained from an official known as the *Gazelus*,[5] who
granted it to Christians on payment of a fixed fee. The wine
itself was rough but good; there was very little choice to be
had. Fortunately it was quite easy to find Muslim traders
ready to sell what they themselves were forbidden to consume. Not only jars or skins of wine, but water too would
have to be carried; not only sacks of smoked meat and
baskets of eggs, but also the utensils and the oil for cooking
them. Dried fish, rice, butter, almonds, raisins, salt and
vinegar helped to provide variety and to give flavour to
bread and the hard dry biscuit that was so difficult to swallow
under conditions of fatigue and thirst. Weariness from
riding an uncomfortable donkey, the monotony of the
trackless desert, the extremes of temperature, all these trials
made it difficult for travellers to relish any food. Those who
had neglected to buy themselves mattresses stuffed with
cotton might find it hard to sleep. Candles and lanterns
too would be necessary to help them bear the "huge loneli-
ness" of the desert in the hours of darkness.

There would be no islands, as in the Mediterranean,
where fresh food and water were easily to be found. It was a
much more serious business to lay in provisions for a journey
through the inland wastes than for a sea voyage; that is one
of the reasons why the pilgrimage to Mount Sinai was

regarded as so very arduous. Even under the most favourable conditions it was likely to take fifteen days each way. Twenty-three years earlier the Spaniard Pero Tafur had borrowed three camels and a mariner's compass, making a dash for it and travelling with minimum equipment,[6] but even that bold adventurer was daunted by his privations and perils. It was a common saying—though not quite accurate—that no pilgrim undertook this journey twice.

In order to persuade the rest of the company that he was not a rich man (and therefore subject to extortionate charges) Roberto decided to wear sombre and travel-stained clothing, and to claim that Guiniforte was not his servant but his nephew. It seems clear that Roberto's arrogance and disgust when he was advised to dress shabbily before landing at Jaffa had given place to a more realistic point of view. He no longer resisted the idea of posing as a person of no importance; he even accepted the situation quite gracefully. Had he not done so, his provisions would have cost him far more than the ordinary bazaar price, he would constantly have had to grant his guides tips and perquisites, and he might well have had to pay "twice as much money to hire the donkeys as it would have cost a local man to buy them outright."[7]

Two of the Brethren of Mount Syon took the opportunity to join Roberto's expedition, for there was business to be transacted with the brethren at Mount Sinai.* Both the brethren chosen for this mission were personal friends of the Milanese pilgrims. One was Fra Francesco of Brescia who had arranged their lodging when they first arrived in Jerusalem; the other an ultramontane whose name is not given but whom Roberto described as "very dear" to them.[8]

---

* Although technically part of the Greek Orthodox Church, the monastery of Mount Sinai at this time accepted the protection of Rome and made a qualified submission to the Holy See; but within a generation the rift had become wide and definite. See below, p. 147.

Bethlehem, of course, came strictly under the jurisdiction of Mount Syon.

II

Roberto's gain of comradeship was Butigella's loss. Without the lively companionship of Fra Francesco, whose home town was near enough to Milan and Pavia for the friends to share many topics of conversation, Butigella found that time hung heavily upon his hands. The library of the brethren was small and unambitious; an intelligent and well-read man like Butigella cannot have found much there to interest him. In the letter he wrote to his brother Giovanni Stefano[9] he mentioned his search for literature to beguile the time. 'When I was left alone with Giovanni Martino", he wrote, "lest I should become a prey to boredom . . . I sought the holy brethren who maintain the Holy Sepulchre . . . and asked them if they would lend me certain books in their possession."[10] One of those he borrowed was the *De redemptione & captione Terrae Sanctae*, a descriptive history of the Holy Land written many years earlier by Jacques de Vitry. Butigella amused himself by making long extracts from this work. He wove them into a *Historia Jerosolomitana*, prefixing to it an interesting dedication to Giovanni Stefano.* When he brought this manuscript home, and had some copies made, the authorship was ascribed to him although nowhere does he claim for it any originality. Just as the writers of guide-books—Wey and others—drew freely upon the common stock of knowledge, so did Butigella in piecing together his extracts from de Vitry's work, that itself owed much to earlier histories. No plagiarism was intended or, indeed, committed.

As Giovanni Martino de Ferrariis improved in health he and Butigella were able to do a little sightseeing together. Indeed, by the time Sanseverino rejoined them after his visits to Mount Sinai and Cairo, they had a good working

* See Appendix B for details.

knowledge of most of the Holy Places in and about Jerusalem.

III

On the last day of July Roberto and Guiniforte bade their friends goodbye. The previous evening word had come to Mount Syon that three new pilgrims had arrived in Jerusalem; for their benefit the Guardian arranged with the Muslim officials for the Church of the Holy Sepulchre to be opened once again. The Milanese slipped in with the newcomers, intent upon spending the night there in preparation for their pilgrimage to Sinai. Early in the morning they made confession and received Holy Communion. Afterwards they spent most of the day resting with Butigella and the invalid until "towards the hour of Vespers, they took leave of the Guardian and the Brethren. With much weeping and tenderness of heart, they embraced and kissed the said d. Giovanni Matteo and m. Giovanni Martino their companions, and also the servants who were to remain behind."[11] At last the emotional farewells were finished; then, "calling upon the name of Our Lord they rode forth from Jerusalem".

It was late in the evening before the party arrived at Bethlehem, where they proposed to stay the night. Like his friends who had visited the place a few weeks earlier, Roberto found the town "very dilapidated". On his first visit he had noted that it was inhabited by "hideous Saracens", but nevertheless it seemed to him that the church at Bethlehem "had formerly been glorious, . . . even now it was still beautiful".[12] The two brethren from Mount Syon were warmly welcomed by the Guardian* who, being a native of Crema near Milan, had much in common with Sanseverino whom he received with "the utmost pleasure".

At dawn the next morning the travellers collected their

---

* His name was Fra Donato.

goods and set out for a resting-place beside a well, about seven miles from Bethlehem. As it was very hot, even at this early hour, the pilgrims plodded on slowly to an inn or *khān* lying beside their route. This was not an inn in the European sense, but a court or enclosure within four walls where it was possible for nomads to camp with all their flocks and herds. This *khān* was ancient and famous, known to generations of travellers as Solomon's Pools. Roberto's company shared this lodging with two caravans that converged upon the *khān* after his party were already established. There was much noise, and much discomfort also from the vermin known as "Pharaoh's lice"; few slept well that night. With a bad stretch of road before them, they made an early start in the hope of covering some forty miles before nightfall. Again it was very hot; again they rested for two hours at mid-day. The pilgrims were all but exhausted when at last, late at night, they reached the city of Gaza (or Gazara), where they camped in comparative comfort. This was the last place of any sophistication that they would visit before beginning their journey across the trackless waste, "where nothing was to be seen save sand and sky".[13] Here at last they were able to relax. Those who still had shopping to do could supply their needs at leisure, for the party stayed on in Gaza until Tuesday, August 8th. Several additional camels had to be found; it was important that these should be Arabian beasts, well accustomed to the ground they were to traverse. In the end eight were chosen to carry wine, water, biscuit, and other provisions, loaded in bales high upon the camels' backs. There were eight donkeys, too, for Roberto and his companions, but Mahomet the Moorish guide preferred to ride a mare.

Roberto seems to have been unusually complaisant; the *Viaggio* at this point is full of praise for the arrangements made by Mahomet and for "the great help and service" provided by Fra Francesco and the Christian interpreter named Jacomo who acted as Mahomet's deputy. There is a new quality about his diary; the first-hand description of his journey from Gaza to St. Catherine's monastery is in many ways the most original part of his narrative. Parted as he was from his close friends Butigella and Giovanni Martino, Roberto wrote down impressions that would ordinarily have been dissipated in conversation; perhaps he found in his journal some solace for his lack of their companionship.

The extra day spent in this outpost was a concession to the Muslims who were celebrating the season of Ramadan, then drawing to its conclusion.* During this ninth month of the Muslim calendar all Muslims fasted between the hours of dawn and sunset, "then, the whole of the night they ate and drank as much and as often as they wished, right up to sunrise on the following day", as Roberto noted under Friday, August 11th. He admired their strength of will and purpose, in facing the rigours of desert travel unfortified during daytime by food or drink. On leaving Gaza Roberto's caravan moved according to the routine generally observed by desert travellers. A start was made some two or three hours before dawn, in order to avoid the greatest heat. At mid-day a 'pavilion' or tent was set up for the riders, while camels and asses were given food and drink. A fully laden camel could not be expected to travel at a faster rate than about two and a quarter miles an hour, the caravan therefore had to be on the move for many hours in order to cover the normal distance of some twenty-five miles. Time must be allowed not only for the travellers to rest but also for the beasts to graze; sometimes it was necessary to search a wide area before enough greenstuff for the animals could be found. Water, too, was scarce and often brackish; one day, after a long search, the party discovered a water hole, "but it tasted so strongly of sulphur that it was absolutely useless", said Roberto in some disgust.

* In 1457 the Muslim's year had begun on November 19th; during the following summer Ramadan ran from July 16th to August 15th.

By the evening of August 8th they had covered some thirty miles. The only excitement had been a glimpse of two light-coloured gazelles and a strange creature that they could not identify as it crossed their path. Roberto described it as "a serpent, large as a cat, long and sinuous, with four feet."[14] As they advanced upon it, the creature disappeared in a scurry of sand, while the pilgrims were left to wonder what it was that they had seen. Despite the description, which suggests a giant lizard, it probably was a jerboa of which there were many in the desert. A French pilgrim passing this way a few years later noticed a number of these, leaping and scuttling this way and that; his impression was that they were the size of young rabbits.[15] Roberto may have been misled by the tremendously long tail.

As he lay in his tent that night, in the deep silence Roberto heard "a strange whistling and sighing"; he was assured by the guides that these sounds were made by "serpents", an ascription that comforted him very little. Seasoned warrior as he was, Roberto must have felt something of the panic fear attributed to Holmes and Dr. Watson as they waited in Stoke Moran for the "deadly swamp adder" to whistle its way through the ventilator and down the bell-rope to attack the infamous Dr. Roylott.* Before many nights had passed, however, the pilgrims had all become accustomed to the stillness; after the fatigues of their travelling they slept the sleep of exhaustion until they were roused in the small hours to rise and continue the journey.

A sharp look-out was kept for Arab raiders. These Bedouin were liable to attack either Turks or Christians without discrimination. Sometimes they could be bought off by presents of food—particularly the biscuit, or hard tack, that they seem to have enjoyed more than did the pilgrims whose staple food it was—but the bands of nomads were still a constant danger. A watch was kept both night

* Described by Sir A. Conan Doyle in *The Adventure of the Speckled Band.*

and day lest they should make a surprise raid. On one occasion the party fell in with a company of Arabs mounted on horses and dromedaries for fast travelling; Roberto described them as "possessing no habitation and no clothes—except a kind of sack that covers their bodies from the shoulders to the knees, with bare arms, and they carry tents that are dark in colour and very small".[16] They belonged to a mountain tribe that ranged the rocky hillsides; Roberto noted with approval that they were perfectly disciplined and obedient to their leaders. Since they lived chiefly on camels' milk, the nomads were delighted to accept a present of biscuits from the pilgrims.

It is not possible to trace the exact route that the caravan took, for there was no established itinerary. The journey to Mount Sinai was taken as a 'point-to-point', avoiding any district where Bedouin activity was suspected at the time. Much of the terrain was a trackless waste; the travellers' main pre-occupation was to find water for themselves and their beasts while they travelled as unobtrusively as possible through the Arab lands. Because Sanseverino does not mention many place-names in the *Viaggio*—practically none that are identifiable—it must be assumed that he was content to put himself in the hands of his guides. Aided by the experienced merchant-traveller Antonio di Franco, Mahomet and Jacomo selected the route that seemed to them the best and safest in the conditions of the moment.[17]

At various points of the journey Roberto's party was associated with other travellers and pilgrims; these drifted together seeking safety and companionship. It is hard to say how many there were in his caravan from day to day, for Roberto's preoccupation was with his immediate associates. The presence of others can only be deduced from casual references; occasionally we read of "the Frenchmen"* or "the party of Sienese" who joined Roberto's homeward voyage, but these were only casual 'ships that

*This did not necessarily mean 'natives of France', see footnote on p. 155.

Giovanni Martino de Ferrariis   Roberto da Sanseverino

John Tiptoft, Earl of Worcester

Venice, *c.* 1400, from *Li Livres du graunt Caam* by Marco Polo

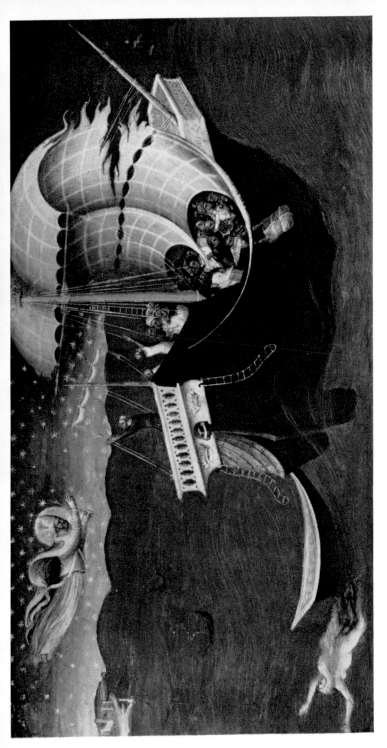

Storm at Sea: St. Nicholas calming the tempest by Lorenzo di Bicci

William Wey's Map (detail)

Largest group of buildings represents Jerusalem.
The Dead Sea at top right

The Holy Sepulchre, from a presentation copy of Capodilista's account
of this pilgrimage

St. Catherine's Chapel on Mount Sinai from the *Pilgrim Book*
of Gabriel Muffel

The Giraffe, from the *Pilgrim Book* of Gabriel Muffel

pass in the night' and never became an integral part of the expedition.

On Sunday, August 13th, the caravan took the road as usual, two hours before dawn. As no water had been found throughout the previous day, it was important to press on to a large oasis known to exist some twenty miles ahead. If, that is, their course was as accurate as they all hoped. As evening fell they rejoiced to see the outline of the mill, worked by two camels, that had been set there by the Sultan to raise water from a deep well. The water was good, and so plentiful that forty or fifty camels could drink at once. Four Arabs were permanently in charge of this oasis, which marked the point where the road to Mount Sinai forked away from the caravan route to Mecca. Antonio di Franco the Calabrian parted from them here, for he was a hard-headed business man intent upon his routine buying in the bazaars; he had neither time nor inclination to visit the shrine of St. Catherine. The pilgrims would now have to go on alone, over rougher and even less frequented country, unsustained by Antonio's cheerful presence and professional knowledge.

Water, when they could find it, tasted of sulphur or worse. Even the reserves carried in jars and skins, now very stale, had become so foul-tasting that neither the pilgrims nor their animals could stomach it. Their spirits were at their lowest ebb when, on Wednesday, August 16th, the party caught sight of Mount Sinai towering upon the horizon. They were approaching the edge of the plain or plateau over which they had been labouring; an escarpment fell away from their feet and a great panorama stretched out before their eyes. All were greatly comforted by the sight of "the mountain of St. Catherine, and that of Moses, greater than all the others" that lay directly before them. Thanking God for His goodness in bringing them so far, they made light of the difficulties and dangers that still had to be overcome.

These were, nevertheless, considerable. Eighty difficult miles still had to be traversed; although in the clear air the mountains seemed near at hand it would be three days at least before the pilgrims reached their lower slopes. On their right hand was a view of the Red Sea; this, too, lay three days' journey distant. Immediately ahead and below was the parched and forbidding valley known to the natives as Debbet-el-Ramla; Roberto made no attempt to record its name but commented on the difficulty of descending the precipitous cliff "in so hot an atmosphere that it was practically insupportable".[18]

Descending into a narrow valley, hemmed in by the rugged hillsides on either hand, the travellers struggled on past high cliffs of red rock and over great boulders that often barred their way. The rocks gave them some shade, there were fissures too and shallow caves where they could shelter from the sun's rays, but this was more than offset by the laborious going and the treacherous surface of pebbles, dust, and scree. Here and there a scrubby bush or emaciated willow-tree proved there was some moisture in the ground, but the pilgrims could find neither water for themselves nor grazing for their beasts. When the wind blew it brought no relief, for the hot air scarifying their faces distressed the pilgrims even more than the scorching stillness. Towards evening the heat became more intense, Roberto said, "with a strong hot wind worse in its effect than any other wind that blows". To crown their misfortunes, the Arab guides now declared that they could not remember the way. There should be a track that they might follow to Mount Sinai (now screened from their view by the intervening hills) but it was hard to find and no one could recall which way it ran. Roberto was exasperated, filled, as he said "with ill will directed against everyone".[19] At this point, however, a young Arab appeared in the distance, riding towards them. He turned out to be a delightful young man with excellent manners—"piacevolissimo", Roberto said—best of all, he knew the district well and was able to tell them which road to take. Indeed, through Jacomo the interpreter, the newcomer told Roberto that he was willing to accompany them all the way to the monastery.

The pilgrims' immediate troubles were now almost at an end. It was decided to leave the camels and stores at the foot of the mountain, since it would be easier to press on without them. On Friday, August 18th, in a final burst of speed the pilgrims reached the gates of the monastery as evening fell. Exhausted as they were by the fatigues and anxieties of their journey, all of them felt exalted and triumphant at reaching their destination. It was the hour of Vespers, but not one of the pilgrims was fit to visit the church that night. The monks entertained them in a large refectory, giving them for food and drink the customary half glass of wine, with bread and salted fish taken from the Red Sea.[20] After supper they rose, one by one they staggered to the lodging provided for them and in a few moments had fallen sound asleep. Their formal thanksgiving must wait until next day.

MOUNT SINAI

> ... thinking to themselves what a long way they had
> come from home in order to see the body of Santa
> Caterina and this holy mountain ... little by little
> they crept up to the top although it took them three
> hours to achieve it.
>
> Roberto da Sanseverino:
> *Viaggio in Terra Santa*, 1458.

The next day was Saturday; the pilgrims rose refreshed
from their long night's sleep and immediately made their
way to the church where the body of St. Catherine lay.
According to legend, angels had carried the saint's body
after her martyrdom* to the Jebel Katherin, one of the peaks
of Mount Sinai. A fresco in the Brera at Milan shows the
angels in flight across the desert with their burden. Later,
her body was transferred to a marble sarcophagus, lower
down the mountain slope, and in the eighth century a little
church was built over the tomb and dedicated to this wise
and outspoken saint. St. Catherine of Alexandria, step-
daughter of the Empress Helena (mother of Constantine
the Great), had been Queen of Egypt from the age of four-
teen. All her delight was in philosophy: she had a splendid
brain and a singular power of persuasive argument. Indeed,
during the persecution of the Christians under Maxentius,
when St. Catherine was pleading their cause, her eloquence
was so impressive that she converted all the learned prosecu-
tors so that they too became Christians and themselves
suffered martyrdom. The Emperor Maxentius, charmed
by Catherine's beauty and courage, wished to marry her,

* In A.D. 317 (November 25th).

but she repudiated him in forthright language, claiming that she was betrothed to Christ. The 'Espousal of St. Catherine' was a favourite subject for painters, from Luini to Correggio; almost always she is represented bearing the symbol of her martyrdom, the 'catherine wheel' that is associated with her name. When she was condemned for her faith to be broken on wheels with sharp spikes, during her martyrdom fire from Heaven shattered the wheels so that they burst into flaming fragments, maiming and scattering the onlookers. So dramatic a climax made the legend of St. Catherine immensely popular; in Italy she was widely known as 'Caterina delle Ruote' (i.e. of the wheels) and everywhere as the patron saint of wheelwrights and mechanics as well as of students, schools and colleges, of spinsters, princesses, and ladies of noble birth.

In this holy chapel Fra Francesco of Brescia celebrated Mass for the pilgrims, "molto divotamente" said Roberto. Afterwards they remained for a while in the church, occupying themselves with their private devotions. When they emerged everyone went into the garden of the monastery, delighting in its unexpected beauty. The garden was extensive—"in length, two bow-shots"*—well watered and full of all kinds of fruit. It was hard to believe that so lush and gracious a garden could exist in such a wilderness. All that day the pilgrims refreshed themselves, wandering in the monastery and its precincts, while the memory of their terrible journey seemed no more than a dream. It was still very warm, but on the mountainside there was air and a fresh breeze very different from the hot sand-laden wind to which they had become accustomed. Roberto admired the great iron gates; he examined, as always, the walls and the fortifications, finding them strong and well built. The church seemed to him to be about the same size as that at Bethlehem, but plainer. He noted with pleasure the statue of Our Lady and the Child Jesus that faced the entrance.

* i.e. Shots from a *balstra*. This might mean from a catapult.

Near at hand Mount Sinai stood up "as red as fire";[1] the pilgrims' thoughts turned to the ascent that they were to make the following day. Immediately after Mass, on Sunday, August 20th, accompanied by Arabs and by some of the monks, they began the wearisome climb. As they plodded up the slopes, slipping and sliding on the treacherous surface, certain of the pilgrims dropped out, sitting down to rest, for they were convinced that they could never reach the summit. Their fellows persuaded them to rise again and press on to complete the last lap, for it would have been sad indeed if they had failed when so near success. Halfway up the mountain they passed a chapel dedicated to Our Lady; finally they reached the little church that marked the place where the angel had first brought the body of St. Catherine before it was translated to its later resting place. This is shown in a charming picture drawn seven years after Sanseverino and his friends halted at the sacred spot; it is in the *Pilgrim Book* of Gabriel Muffel of Nuremberg, a manuscript now in the British Museum.[2] The chapel is perched on a precipitous Mount Sinai, with the monastery at its foot, all the buildings, and the tall trees of the garden, enclosed within walls pierced only by the iron gates that had so impressed Roberto.

The pilgrims visited also the other holy places of the mountain, "particularly the spot where Our Lord God gave the tables of the law to Moses, and the place where He appeared to him in the burning bush".[3] They noted, too, the rock whence water miraculously gushed forth "and to this day runs ever down the mountain side". The return journey was painful and slow, for by now the pilgrims' aching muscles would hardly allow them to put one foot in front of another. Leg weary and footsore as they were, the pilgrims made their way back to the monastery with their minds at ease, in a glow of achievement.

Next day they paid a further visit to the church, to inspect the bones of St. Catherine and to make their offerings at her shrine beneath the high altar. Every man gave as generously as he could, for it was obvious that a large sum was needed to keep up a monastery in so remote a spot, to provide also hospitality for pilgrims and the doles of food with which the monks tried to buy the goodwill of the Bedouin tribesmen in the neighbourhood. The Greek churches in Rhodes, Cyprus, Crete and Corfu all sent contributions for its upkeep; donations came too from individuals throughout Europe. Representative of these is the silver-gilt chalice presented by Charles VI of France that is still one of the monastery's treasures.

The monks were often known as Caloyers, to show their distinction as exponents of the Greek rite; Canon Pietro Casola's version was *calogeri*,[4] but the less-educated Sanseverino's spelling of *chaloyri* was nearer the original.[5] They observed their vow of poverty with the utmost severity, rejecting meat of all kinds, living on eggs, cheese, and the produce of the garden Roberto so greatly admired. Their habits were coarse and threadbare; they slept on the floor of cells made of mud and reeds. Thirty years later a Dominican from Ulm[6] complained of the meanness of these monks, asserting that they charged the pilgrims a penny each for the hire of staves to help them up the mountain track, made them pay for any water that they used, and refused to lend this Friar Felix a pair of boots. Sanseverino, however, says nothing to bear out such assertions. Critical as he often was, for the *chaloyri* he has nothing but praise in his admiration of their asceticism. The monks of St. Catherine's had formerly acknowledged the authority of Rome; it was not until the latter part of the fifteenth century that the effects of friction between East and West here became acute. It may well be that Roberto, as a layman, was unaware of the dissension that later offended Felix and his friends. At all events he was grateful for the hospitality provided at the monastery; he seems to have enjoyed his visit very much, although he complained two days later of legs still aching from the rough climb. The two Franciscan brethren stayed on to complete their business; Roberto was sorry to lose the companionship of Fra Francesco who had proved so good a friend.

Three hours before sunrise, on Tuesday, August 22nd, the pilgrims were on their way home. They found the donkeys and camels with their drivers in the sheltered spot where they had been waiting for the pilgrims' return. It then seemed to be a simple matter to make their way across the boulder-strewn plain and to climb the escarpment they had descended so precariously a week earlier, but the march was a long one; it was midnight before they set up their camp. Already a strong wind was blowing; as the hours slipped by it increased in force until it whipped the tent-pegs from the ground and carried away the 'pavilion' from above the campers' heads. There was no more rest for anyone that night; surrounded by confusion and darkness, in a very ill temper, Roberto and his companions gathered together their possessions and set out through the storm, eyes and nostrils tingling from the harsh grains of sand that filled the air. By dawn the wind had dropped; soon it was hotter than ever before. The climb up the zig-zag path to the crest of the escarpment seemed endless, nevertheless they pressed on doggedly. When at last the party reached the oasis, where they had paused on their outward journey, troubles were soon forgotten. Everything was bustle and excitement, for two caravans were there before them, one heading in either direction. In all, there were upwards of a hundred camels encamped within the enclosure, moaning and snuffling as camels will, while their drivers shouted at one another in tongues incomprehensible to the Europeans. From this point their route diverged from the course they had taken on the outward journey, for now they were making for Cairo and perhaps more distant regions.

The following day, a Friday, the pilgrims sighted the Red Sea and hastened towards its shore. They covered

fifty miles that day* so that on the morrow they found themselves at the water's edge. Soon they were bathing and resting
on the sand, a far more refreshing experience than their ritual
bathe in the waters of the River Jordan. Sunday, August
27th, saw the party striking camp four hours before daybreak;
they made an early start also the next day. The going was
much easier now, for they were on a regular caravan route;
indeed, they met several caravans, all of them making for
Mecca. Roberto was particularly interested in this traffic—
for if he were to fulfil his ambition to extend his explorations
as far as India, this was the road he would expect to take.

It was clear to the pilgrims that they had reached the
fringe of the desert country they had traversed for so long.
Their surroundings suddenly became more civilized, for
they began to pass through villages where they noted on
either hand substantial houses and gardens. Presently they
reached Matariya, the Arabic el-Matariyeh. Here, they
paused to refresh themselves with the pure water from its
holy well, while they recalled the legend of its origin and
of the Garden of Balm that surrounded it. Roberto describes
the Holy Family halting here during the flight into Egypt.[7]
Our Lady was said to have left Jesus lying on the ground
while she went to the village to ask for water; on her return
she found a spring of the purest water welling up near His
feet, where His little heels had drummed upon the ground.
Rejoicing in its abundance, Mary took the opportunity
to wash the Holy Child's tiny shirts, soiled and travel-
stained by the long journey. "Where these were hung to
dry upon the bushes, there was born the balm that is found
nowhere else in the world."[8]

Other legends claimed that the bushes of balm had
originally been brought from India by the Queen of Sheba
on her visit to King Solomon, and that later they were
transplanted in Egypt, but Roberto records only the

---

* This seems an extremely long journey, but that is what Roberto says.
The party accomplished upwards of forty miles on several other occasions.

association with the Holy Family. The precious balsam plants* were recognized as the Sultan's personal property; he derived a useful income from the oil extracted from them. The Sultan and the richer Mamluks had built themselves handsome villas around Matariya, which was only four miles from Cairo and a convenient retreat from city life. The gardens had gazebos or belvederes (or more homely summer-houses) with extensive views across the foreground of shrubs and trees to the desert beyond. The copious water had been conducted to a splendid bath-house, large enough, it was said, to accommodate three hundred bathers.

In the Garden of Balm, where the pilgrims were allowed to walk—although forbidden to take surreptitious cuttings or even to crush the leaves in their fingers—Roberto noticed also a magnificent fig tree. This, too, was a subject for veneration, for it was said to have provided in its hollow trunk a refuge for the Child Jesus. There was fruit here of every kind, dates and many other trees "gientili et belli". The holy well was a great basin bordered with a curb of the purest white marble; two oxen worked the wheel drawing up water to irrigate the Garden of Balm. On Saturdays no water could be used because the oxen refused to work— "not for anything would they turn the wheel". This, Roberto said, was another "grande mirachulo".⁹

Here in Matariya the pilgrims rested at ease while they added up the plenary indulgences that they had gained. They feasted on the local-grown fruit and vegetables, new bread and eggs and cheese. No longer would they have to chew the 'hard tack' with aching jaws, no longer huddle into stuffy tents to escape the scorching sandstorms without. A new and agreeable prospect opened before them, for they were about to visit the most gorgeous and famous of Eastern cities; they looked forward with excitement to surrendering themselves to its opulent and exotic charms.

* Botanically speaking, *Commiphora opobalsamum*, a native of S.W. Arabia and Somaliland.

14

CAIRO

In your desire to mingle divine with human matters, you have been to visit the Holy Land and Mount Sinai, and being in Cairo you contemplated penetrating into India.

Paolo Ramusio, dedicatory letter to Sanseverino*

I

At this point Roberto was able to pay off the camel drivers and bid them farewell, for they would no longer be needed. He admitted very fairly that they had served him well, both in finding water for men and beasts and in managing their awkward animals with practised skill. Hereafter the baggage, like the pilgrims themselves, must be carried on mules and asses.[1]

The pilgrims had expected that the Khalif (or 'Sultan') would send his interpreter† out from Cairo to interview them at Matariya. For some reason, however, this official did not come. Roberto therefore decided to dispatch his own interpreter, Mahomet, to Cairo in order to make the necessary arrangements for licences and permits, instructing him also to find a house where Roberto and Guiniforte could lodge. Mahomet went off early on Monday morning; Roberto followed at his leisure the next day, August 29th.

---

* Prefixed to his vernacular translation of Roberto Valturio's *De Re Militari*, Verona 1483.

† The term 'interpreter' has been preferred to Roberto's "Truciman" or dragoman because the modern meaning of this term might be misleading in the context.

The road lay "always through gardens" and they paused
from time to time to admire these and to view the exciting
sky-line of the domes and minarets of the city lying spread
before them. As the sun set the party reached the suburbs;
for the last two miles of their journey they passed through
great crowds and were lucky to meet their guide Mahomet
who led them swiftly to their lodging.

As soon as they were established, the two Milanese
hurried out into the streets to see what they could of the
sights before darkness fell. After two hours they returned
to their quarters greatly impressed by the size and magnificence of Cairo. It seemed to them "more than four times
the size of Milan"; indeed, Roberto thought that the whole
population of Rome, Venice, Milan and Florence could have
been housed there and still there would have been room for
more.[2] He was not singular in this impression; it was the
extent as well as the richness of the city that always
astonished visitors. More than a hundred years earlier a
Muslim from Morocco had journeyed thither along the
Nile; he wrote in the journal of his travels:[3] "I arrived at
length at Cairo, mother of cities . . . mistress of broad
regions and fruitful lands, boundless in multitude of buildings, peerless in beauty and splendour, the meeting place
of comer and goer. . . whose throngs surge as the waves of
the sea, and can scarce be contained in her for all her size
and capacity." If Roberto's description is less flowery, that
is because he was no practised reporter, but it leaves his
readers in no doubt about his wonder and admiration.

This was the Cairo described in the *Arabian Nights*; the
thousand and one tales of Shahrazad reflect the ideas,
fashions, manners, trade, notions of justice, and above all
the architecture and the mode of living in this city during
the later Middle Ages.* The mosques and the mausoleums,
the courtyards with their green trees, the heavy iron grilles

* Although the compiler of these tales sets them in Baghdad during the
reign of Harun al Rashid (786-809), the contemporary of Charlemagne.

over the windows of the houses, the ceramic mosaics of
Persian faience let in to the carved plaster of the walls, the
stucco rose windows[4]—all these were new and exciting to
Western eyes. "The chief streets", Roberto wrote, "are
well furnished with all sorts of things, but not in the manner
of ours, nor do they have such beautiful houses . . . theirs
are all of stone, . . . their ceilings are of gold and blue and
they have many carpets." He found the houses airy and well
arranged to suit the climate, but thought the courts might
be draughty when the *tramontana* wind was blowing. The
coloured glass of the windows, glowing like fire when light
shone through them, fascinated Western pilgrims as they
roamed the streets by night. Oil lamps burned in the
towers, or swung on poles thrust out of windows or inter-
stices in every minaret; many houses had lanterns hanging
above their doors. Only Venice at times of festival could
compete with this illumination; to Europeans—and particularly to northerners—it was indeed a revelation. A Frenchman once declared that in Cairo "as much oil is burnt as
they drink wine at Orleans".[5]

The evening of Wednesday, August 30th, Roberto went
to call upon the Ambassador from Rhodes, in the hope that
he would help him make arrangements for visiting the
Sultan. Now that they had arrived in Cairo Roberto found
Mahomet the interpreter very elusive; he seemed to take
no further interest in the pilgrims or their plans. Indeed,
Roberto remarked that he could not imagine why Fra
Francesco of Brescia had recommended Mahomet so
highly,[6] for he found him quite useless. The Ambassador
proved helpful as well as friendly; he promised to take
Roberto and Guiniforte Smagioso with him three days later
to call on the Sultan in the 'Castello', or Citadel, where he
dwelt with his wives and bodyguard, and courtiers drawn from
the Mamluks or ruling class. The interesting thing about
the Mamluks was that they were descendants of freed slaves,
mostly Circassians, who had won power and riches, and at

this date supplied Khalifs* for Cairo and all Egypt.[7] They had already held power for two centuries when Roberto made his visit. Mamluk rule would last another sixty years before crumbling in the face of the Ottoman Turks— conquerors of Constantinople in 1453—who then extended their influence over the whole country of Egypt.

The two days before his promised visit to the Citadel were spent by Roberto in an energetic tour of Babylon (old Cairo), the Nile, and the Pyramids. He and Guiniforte hired horses, taking with them a Dominican friar, who had lived in Cairo for four years, to act as guide, as well as an official interpreter named Tambeccho.[8] Like most medieval travellers, who used to refer to the Pyramids as the 'barns of Joseph', Roberto accepted the theory that these were, as he says,[9] "the Pharaoh's granaries". He compared them to "the tomb of Romulus at Rome"; presumably he was thinking of the Pyramid of Cestius. An Irish pilgrim, seeing the Pyramids for the first time, thought that "they look more like the summits of mountains than repositories of corn";[10] Roberto remarked only their height, then turned to a description of the River Nile. Immediately opposite Babylon was the island of Rōda where, according to Arab tradition, Pharaoh's daughter had found Moses. Like all good pilgrims the two Milanese set foot upon the island, then listed it as one of the sites that had duly been examined. Roberto and his party rode for five miles along the river bank: "everywhere it was inhabited by innumerable people. Moreover, so many boats were on the river that no one who had not seen it would have believed it possible."

On his way back from this expedition Roberto and his servant called again on the Ambassador from Rhodes in order to make final arrangements for their visit to the Sultan next day. The Ambassador lent the Milanese two long garments, appropriate wear for this occasion. He

* As Roberto always refers to "the Sultan" rather than the Khalif, this description (although it is inexact) is retained elsewhere to avoid confusion.

warned them to present themselves at his house an hour
before dawn. Roberto and Guiniforte were careful to arrive
punctually. Together with the Ambassador their friend,
some miscellaneous Western pilgrims,* some Knights of
Rhodes and two more ambassadors from Cyprus, they all
set out on horseback, accompanied by the interpreters
and Mamluks that the Sultan had sent to form an escort.
"Passing through no fewer than fifteen wrought-iron gates,
past courtyards and houses of surpassing beauty where the
Mamluks dwell",[11] they came at last to a great open court
"twice the size of the one at Milan", where the Sultan
"reclined upon a little bed, surrounded by his counsellors
and noble lords". Ten Mamluks, dressed in pure white,
stood on either side to form a guard of honour for the
ambassadors and all their company. It was, said Roberto,
a noble sight to see, as were the combats staged for their
pleasure. These lasted a full hour. Afterwards the Sultan
entertained his guests with conversation, through his
interpreters. Finally they made reverence to him, then
passed on to visit his son. Gifts of robes were made to the
ambassadors, but the rest of the party had to be content
with a conducted tour round the citadel and the singularly
beautiful view that they enjoyed from its ramparts.[12]

This stronghold was set on a hill, known as El Jebel
(i.e. the mountain), that dominated the whole city and the
surrounding countryside. Already, when Saladin came to
Cairo as Governor of Egypt in 1169, he had found the
beginnings of a castle and military barracks on this site,
but his was the vision of a new Cairo crowned by the most
magnificent of fortresses. During the eight years Saladin
spent in the city he raised it from a provincial town to the
same status as Damascus. Not only was he the embodiment

---

* These are described as "Franchi", but—as Roberto himself explains,
Viaggio, p. 148, this does not mean 'Frenchmen' but merely 'Westerners'.
It is interesting to note that when Henry Layard was travelling in the Near
and Middle East four hundred years later, he was called a Feringhi (Frank).

of all the chivalrous virtues and a mighty general—as the leaders of the Third Crusade found to their cost—Saladin showed himself to be a great town-planner, a builder with civilized tastes, and a discriminating patron of craftsmen of all races. In following the tradition of the great Crusader castles of Syria he took all that was best from their design, erecting his towering fortress as the apex of his defensive work in extension of the city walls.[13] Roberto could appreciate the strength and beauty of the Citadel to the full; this was something he really understood. He was fascinated, too, by the weapons and engines of war that he saw displayed within, infinitely preferring them to the jewels and treasures that attracted most of the tourists. Roberto's interest in war machines, however fantastic in design, was well known to his contemporaries; it was for this reason that Paolo Ramusio dedicated to him a translation of Roberto Valturio's textbook on the subject.* These machines at Cairo, built for the Mamluk Sultan, were—as might be expected—more exotic and elaborate than those Roberto had seen at Rhodes.

Before leaving the Citadel, where the visitors had been shown every evidence of the Sultan's splendour, power, and glory, they were led to a great open piazza where more than six hundred mounted Mamluks were drawn up, waiting to begin their game of *lanza*. In general principle this was a kind of polo; it was very exciting for both players and spectators. An Irish monk who witnessed the game made some interesting notes about it. "All Saracen horsemen ride after the fashion of women," he wrote, "on low saddles and with short stirrups, to the front of which is fixed a ring, in which is placed a club or mace for the defence of the rider." Of the rules of the game this Brother Symon

* The *De Re Militari*, in 12 books. Some of the machines Valturio designed were actually made, by two brothers named Barocci. One that was built a few years later still exists in the Museum at Urbino. Roberto himself does not seem to have used any of these 'engines' in his campaigns—except the three *gatti* he employed to shield his men at the battle of Figarolo in 1482.

says: "The game they play resembles very closely that played by shepherds in Christian lands with a ball and curved sticks, with this exception, that the Sultan and his nobles never strike the ball unless they are on horseback. . . . And without doubt in this game many horses and knights are injured, and rendered unfit for active service in the future."[14] Sometimes the Sultan himself played when there was a great concourse of spectators, "who . . . watch the game and especially the exploits of the Sultan; and whenever he should strike the ball, the spectators all cheer and praise him, sounding innumerable trumpets and striking countless harsh kettle-drums."[15]

The Mamluks were marvellous horsemen; Roberto was greatly impressed by their skill. He praised not only their riding but also their dexterity in the use of all kinds of weapons. It seems that Roberto's whole attitude to the Muslims had greatly changed now that he knew them better; in his *Viaggio* they are no longer Saracen dogs to be despised and avoided, but individuals worthy of respect or even admiration.

Roberto had already consulted the Ambassador from Rhodes about his proposed journey to India; now was his opportunity to discuss the matter further with the friendly Mamluks. The advice given him was not encouraging. Roberto began to realize that the difficulties were greater than he had imagined, for the privations of his desert journey were still fresh in his mind. He found, too, that the distances to be traversed would be immense. General opinion seemed to be that he had better return to Jerusalem in order to make his way from there to Damascus, where it would be easier to find guides and first-hand information. This Roberto resolved to do.

II

The time had now come for the Milanese to pack up their belongings and to take leave of their Muslim hosts. After the polo game, on the way back to their lodging, Roberto and Guiniforte paused to call at various houses with the intention of saying goodbye to those who had befriended them. It was very hot; more than ever the streets were thronged with people. After the Milanese had forced their way home through the crowds they were completely exhausted. However, by the time of Vespers they found themselves able to set out again, and after a good night's rest they were ready to spend two more days in sightseeing.

On September 4th Roberto had his first view of a giraffe. This "zaraffa", as he called it, was immensely tall, "white skinned with red spots; it is lower at the rear end than at the front. It has a supple neck of three arms' length, a long head with a pointed nose, eyes that are large and rather like those of an ox, large ears like a cow's, on the top of its head two little horns like those of a young goat."[16] Roberto's description is more accurate—if less picturesque—than that of the Florentine Simone Sigoli. To him, "the giraffe is almost like an ostrich save that its chest has no feathers but has very fine white wool . . . it has horse's feet and bird's legs . . . the head is like a horse's and is white, and it has two horns like a wether, and it eats barley and bread like a horse . . . it is really a very deformed thing to see."[17] It was impossible to see an elephant "because, of the two that used to be there, one was dead and the Sultan had sent the other one away". Nor was Roberto able to find any tigers, although he heard that some were in captivity and were occasionally on view.

Tuesday, September 5th, was taken up with final preparations for the journey to Jerusalem, the issue of licences and the stamping of permits. All formalities went through very easily, thanks to the good offices of the Ambassador from Rhodes. The other *Franchi*, or European pilgrims (among them the two Knights of Rhodes), were also aiming for Jerusalem; it seemed natural and convenient for Roberto to join their party. At sunrise on Wednesday, therefore,

he and Guiniforte left their lodging early in order to reach
the rendezvous. Roberto remarked ruefully that "in departing it was necessary to pay sums of money to many people
who had not performed the slightest service, some of whom
we had not even seen; and with great fatigue and expense
did we leave them".[18] There would be more fatigue and
even more expense before the pilgrims found themselves
on board a ship bound for Venice; just now, however, they
had so great a store of memories of the strange sights,
sounds and smells that they had encountered that this did
not seem to be the time for counting the cost. Had Roberto
suffered such extortion five weeks earlier, before he left
for Sinai, there would probably have been a great outcry,
but there can be no doubt that he had mellowed during this
time, developing a new tolerance and understanding of these
age-old Eastern customs.

As they plunged into the sandy desert, where the Children
of Israel had wandered for forty years, the pilgrims kept a
sharp look-out for the Bedouins who might try to ambush
them. The only people they saw, however, were Mamluks
returning from a game of polo and others with falcons on
their fists, until they overtook a caravan that they joined
for company. The slow-moving camels so delayed their
progress that, after a leisurely halt at Matariya, they went
no further than "Chanico" that night. This town, that
seemed to Roberto to be "about the size of Monza", was
probably Kanis. Here they spent the night, amid delightful
gardens, about twelve miles from Cairo.

Next day the pilgrims parted company with the caravan,
pressing on to make up for lost time. They skirted the desert,
delighting in the "beautiful tract of country . . . rich in
corn and flowers"[19] that led them to Belbeis. Here they sat
in the shade of date palms beside a spring, while Roberto
ran his eye over the neat and prosperous town, full of all
the provisions necessary for travellers. Here you could
buy food of many kinds; here you could hire camels or

asses for your journey. Roberto compared it with Lodi[20] (on the Via Emilia near Milan). He and his party were fortunate in finding a *khan*, where they lodged comfortably until morning. Thereafter they followed a well-worn track, meeting travellers heading in both directions, until they reached the village of Katiŷeh, halfway between Cairo and Gaza, where a number of routes met. Here a tribute was collected; all the pilgrims paid their dues without questioning or complaint.

From this point on, their road lay over soft loose sand, so that the donkeys sank into it above their hocks and became very distressed. What water they did find was warm and brackish; for three days they seemed to have reverted to the conditions that had governed their journey across the Tîh desert to Sinai. At last, on Thursday, September 14th, Roberto realized that they were nearing Gaza. He recognized the *khan* where they had stayed before branching off towards Mount Sinai; both he and Guiniforte were glad enough to rest there although they were disturbed by a number of Arabs who clamoured for money, biscuit, "and anything else they thought they might obtain".[21]

While the rest of the party continued on their way to Jerusalem, Roberto, his servant, and the two Knights of Rhodes turned aside to spend a day in the wilderness where St. John the Baptist had dwelt. It was necessary to have guides for this expedition, since it would be easy to lose the way or to stumble into many kinds of trouble. Over boulders and rocks they scrambled, ascending a narrow valley that lay between two mountains to the spot where a torrent gushed out of the hillside: this was the holy place where St. John baptized believers with water from the stream. All round the church built there in commemoration of St. John were splendid gardens and fruit trees; as the water rushed down to the plain below it irrigated the soil on either side so that Roberto could remark that "all this land in the valley is exceedingly beautiful, full of vines and fruit-bearing trees, with the mildest air imaginable".²² Presently they came to a large village ("the size of Borgo San Donino")* where everyone dismounted to rest a while.

As the sun rose on September 16th they began the last stage of their journey back to Bethlehem, where they arrived at six o'clock in the evening. To his great joy Roberto found that Giovanni Matteo Butigella had come from Jerusalem to meet him; "they embraced one another countless times" before hastening to the church to give thanks for Roberto's safe return. He had been away two days short of seven weeks;† as his experiences crowded into that time had done something to re-shape his character and had added much to his knowledge, it is not surprising that he and Butigella found "an infinite number of things" to talk about. Then Roberto and his man took the road again, for they wanted to arrive in Jerusalem that night. The Knights of Rhodes stayed on in Bethlehem in company with Butigella, in order to visit the church once more for an all-night vigil. In Jerusalem Roberto greeted affectionately Giovanni Martino, now all but recovered from his illness; he then hurried to the Church of Our Lady "to give thanks to God for allowing them to return, safe and in good health, and to beg Him to extend His protection so that they might reach home in Italy without any ill-fortune by the way".²³

* The charming little town on the Via Emilia between Parma and Piacenza. It is now known as Fidenza.

† From August 1st to September 16th.

HOMEWARD BOUND

. . . thankynge Almyghty God with all our hertes of ye grete grace that he gave vnto vs to se and vysyte the sayde blessyd places and holy cytie ones in our lyues or thanne we dyed.

Pylgrymage of Sir Richard Guylforde, 1506

I

Sanseverino was delighted to find Giovanni Martino de Ferrariis so nearly recovered from his illness: "after they had embraced one another they set out to visit the Brothers of Mount Syon", where they met a joyous welcome. As soon as possible the three Milanese went into conference concerning the best means of returning home. Roberto had decided against extending his travels eastward; he would not even go to Damascus to confer with Loredan, who had sent a message pointing out that the Venetian merchants there were still so preoccupied with their affairs that they would not be able to sail for several weeks to come. Roberto now wanted to reach home as quickly as possible. His main reason was the news he had just heard from the Cypriot ambassadors of the death of King Alfonso of Aragon. This great king, who years earlier had won the throne of Naples with the backing of Milan, left only Ferrante, an illegitimate son, to carry on his government. It was clear that a rival claimant, an Angevin prince actively supported by France, had almost as good a claim to the kingdom as had Ferrante. There was thus every likelihood of a war in which Milan might easily become involved.

Roberto felt strongly that he should be close to his uncle the Duke in such a time of crisis, when his professional services could well be needed.

Now that he wished to make definite plans it was particularly galling to Roberto that he was unable to find transport for his party. Ser Antonio Loredan was as unhelpful as Mahomet had been in Cairo; he failed to answer letters, there was no sign of the goods Roberto had asked him to send. Thrown as he was upon his own resources, Roberto found himself frustrated also by the smooth evasiveness of the Syrian shipping agents in Jerusalem. Never a persuasive or diplomatic person, Roberto tried to hector his way into a contract for the return voyage, but to no avail. Fra Francesco of Brescia was no longer at his elbow to translate for him; even those who had a few words of Italian could make nothing of Roberto's Milanese speech. He discovered that the ambassadors from Cyprus proposed to sail from Alexandria. Had Roberto joined their company he could have returned immediately, but he was unwilling to part from his friends, preferring to wait until Giovanni Martino had recovered sufficiently to face the homeward journey. Like many doctors Giovanni Martino was timid where his own health was concerned; in the end he could not bring himself to venture home that year. Instead, he decided to stay on at Mount Syon with the brethren, until the next party of pilgrims should arrive in the spring.

There was no other course for Sanseverino and Butigella to take but to secure passages in the first ship they could find. Roberto decided to go to Acre, hoping to find a captain there who would be willing to take them as passengers. Before leaving Mount Syon the two friends had made some further expeditions to the Holy Places, revisiting Jericho, and washing their hands in the Dead Sea. Finally, they passed yet another night in the Church of the Holy Sepulchre before bidding Giovanni Martino and the

brethren an affectionate farewell. With "the greatest
tenderness and friendship" and "many kisses, tears, and
sighs" the Milanese—together with the two Knights of
Rhodes—took their leave, riding off upon their mules at
midnight on Monday, September 25th.

All this delay and disappointment had a dire effect upon
Roberto's temper and outlook. He reverted to his former
attitude, writing angrily in the *Viaggio* that "it seemed a
thousand years before we got out of the hands of those
Saracen dogs".[1] After the mules had carried them about
fifteen miles on their journey Roberto's spirits to some extent
revived. Leaving the site of the beheading of St. John the
Baptist on their right hand, they passed on the left the
hillside where Our Lady frantically sought for the Child
Jesus before she found Him in the Temple. Soon they were
riding through delightful country "as lovely as it was
fruitful, covered with olive trees bearing a heavy crop . . .
about half a mile further on they found the well where
Our Lord was resting when he spoke with the woman from
Samaria". Then the party reached Napulosa, where Roberto
declared that he was "tormented . . . by those Saracens,
diabolical men" who seem to have demanded illegal tolls.
Once Napulosa lay behind them, the fruitful plains gave
way to steep mountainsides where the going was difficult
and where the craggy rocks gave shelter to nomad tribesmen.
One narrow valley was ill-famed for "the many robberies
and homicides perpetrated by these Arabs":[2] the pilgrims
had to negotiate the path in single file, in fear of their lives.
"Commending themselves to Our Lord God, Signor Roberto
and dom. Giovanni Matteo with great terror and in great
peril, passed through this place without hindrance. And that
same evening, at the setting of the sun, they came to the
house of some Venetian merchants in the city of Acre." The
journey over arid desert and stony mountains at last was
finished: before them lay the sea, smooth and calm at present,
with no suggestion of the stormy voyage that was still to come.

II

Three days had passed since the party quitted Jerusalem but not for another fortnight would they be able to leave Acre. On September 28th Roberto began negotiations with a captain named Francesco di Alberto to secure passages for them all. The Knights of Rhodes naturally wished to disembark on their own island, but Francesco would not promise to call there, nor even to put in at Cyprus where the knights could have found further transport. He categorically refused to take his ship to Beirut in order to join the convoy organized by Loredan. Roberto was angered no less by the captain's intransigence, than by the fares he asked, which seemed inordinately high.[3] The Milanese sought help from their Venetian hosts "who offered them fair words, but did little to help the situation". On Friday morning a messenger arrived from Damascus, bringing letters from the Consul and from Loredan himself. Once again the *patrono* warned Roberto that Alvise Beltramo the pirate was still at large, strongly urging him to travel aboard the *Leza*. Roberto was unable to reconsider his plans, for he was now committed to sailing with Francesco di Alberto, with whom he had already signed a contract witnessed by the Venetian Consul* in Acre.

Francesco promised to leave port within a day or two: in the event this assurance proved as worthless as Loredan's guarantee that the sweetmeats and confectionery Roberto had ordered were actually on their way from Damascus. The Knights of Rhodes went off in dudgeon to make their own arrangements; Butigella and Sanseverino awaited the captain's convenience, their impatience mounting as the days sped by. A party of Sienese pilgrims arrived in Acre at about this time; they too agreed to sail with Francesco di Alberto, but arranged an independent contract. Like the

---

* D. Jeronimo Gabriele. The other witnesses were two Venetian merchants. Roberto paid a deposit amounting to one ducat, twenty *dremi*.

Milanese, they were anxious to reach home as soon as possible. The captain, for his part, vowed that he would be away the moment he could be sure of a favourable wind. Yet, a fortnight later his ship still lay in harbour. Scarcely a breeze ruffled the water or brought relief to the pilgrims who were already embarked in their uncomfortable quarters. Some were suffering from fever, others from dysentery: all were a prey to frustration and boredom.

It was an unhappy company that put to sea on Tuesday, October 10th. Both the Milanese were ill with fever and headache; to both of them the sailors' cries "seemed as though they came from Hell". Of the crew, "enough evil can never be said", Roberto wrote at the height of his misery. In his more fair-minded moments he admitted that the ship, though small, was newly built and well-found, but throughout the voyage he continued to lament the lack of amenities he had taken for granted aboard the *Loredana*. It is true that Roberto was a sick man with a dis-ordered digestive system, but even so, if half his charges were true, the diet in Francesco's ship was bad indeed. There was not enough bread, and what there was proved to be very old and full of worms. The biscuit was "cattivo", in no way to be distinguished from the blackened wood they used for fuel. The water was filthy and insufficient. The little wine they had was much adulterated; the Milanese found a sailor in possession of a private barrel of red wine, some of which he agreed to sell them "at a great price". But it turned out to be black and "so thick that one could cut it with a knife";[4] moreover, it had so terrible a stink that it infected the whole galley. "It would have been better to drink medicinal rhubarb," he wrote in disgust.

It was one of the stipulations in their contract that the pilgrims should have every facility for cooking and serving their own meals. In practice, however, Roberto's servants met difficulty in finding cooking vessels of any kind. They were also at their wits' end in trying to concoct anything that would be if not palatable at least edible. It had not been possible to supplement their diet by buying provisions in Acre, beyond a few chickens, limited quantities of beef and fresh vegetables, hard biscuit and unleavened bread. For the rest they had to rely upon the food provided on board, that was not, as may easily be imagined, consumable by invalids. Most of the cooking devolved upon the German Martin, for Giov' Antonio Drella—hitherto the mainstay of the party—followed the example of Butigella and Roberto himself in casting himself prone upon his bunk the moment there was any motion. "So terrified was he of the sea and of its slightest movement that, as soon as they were under sail, he became so ill that he could not look after his masters or even wait upon himself."[5] Guiniforte and the other servants were not much better; all of them were sea-sick whenever the ship rolled in the trough of high waves. The most useful would have been Calistano who had some experience of illness from his careful nursing of Giovanni Martino, but he had stayed behind in Jerusalem with his master. Faithful Martin had to be steward, valet, and cook at one and the same time, also the bearer of demands and complaints, and general pacificator.

All their medical supplies, too, had been turned over to Giovanni Martino de Ferrariis in Jerusalem, for the Milanese had thought that they would be able to find replacements at Acre. They were, therefore, dependent upon the remedies doled out to them by the barber-surgeon Messer Marco Schiavo, a Venetian subject, who had been retained by Francesco di Alberto as ship's surgeon for this voyage. The pilgrims were, as a matter of fact, very fortunate in having at their service a doctor with first-hand experience of the kind of maladies they might be expected to suffer, for most ships had no medical staff at all. In his feverish state Roberto was scathing about Messer Marco's qualifications and abilities,[6] claiming that he used his instruments "much as a donkey playing the guitar", but the fact remains that all his patients were on the road to recovery by the time the voyage started, and by the second day out most of them were on their feet again.

III

On Friday, October 13th, the ship was well out to sea, travelling fast with a following wind. Over the weekend, however, this freshened to a gale so that by Tuesday all the pilgrims were again suffering "tribulation". Francesco di Alberto, although he seems to have been a moderately good seaman in normal circumstances, became emotional in times of stress. As the storm gathered force, and everyone began to fear that the ship would founder, Roberto noticed that "tears were welling from his eyes, tears of the greatest magnitude". Towards evening on the Wednesday, Roberto suggested that they might repeat the procedure that had produced so happy a result on the outward voyage. He wrote saints' names on slips of paper that he handed to the pilgrims, who took the appropriate vows of making offerings at special shrines. They then cast the slips overboard. At a later stage in the voyage several pilgrims, Roberto among them, made further vows of a pilgrimage to the shrine of Santa Maria Artone, and others to Our Lady of Loreto. Roberto does not record the names of the saints drawn either by himself or by Butigella on October 18th, but he certainly promised to visit Loreto, for he was at great pains to do so when the opportunity came to him six weeks later.

Within a few days of the storm, a fierce argument arose between the captain, the ship's officers, the crew, and the passengers as to the exact whereabouts of the ship. Everyone had his own opinion; few hesitated to voice their views. Some thought that they could discern land, others said it was a cloud effect; when the next morning they discovered that it was land indeed, the wind shifted and blew them rapidly away from it. After much "anguish and tribulation" they found themselves off the island of Scarpant. They were now in a definite shipping lane, where they encountered several vessels of a friendly character, none of whom had seen the corsair Alvise Beltramo.

On the last day of October, a Tuesday, the dreaded wind, the *'garbino'** that had already threatened the ship with destruction, again began to blow. Francesco had no mind to face out the oncoming storm, so he turned off-course towards the port of Mello, in one of the islands of the Greek Archipelago, where he could ride at anchor until the *garbino* should abate. This was one of a dozen islands under the rule of a Venetian patrician named Giovanni Crispi, who held the title of Duke of the Archipelago. Both crew and passengers longed to get ashore so that they could buy provisions and other much-needed gear. Most of them had been without meat, or wine, or cheese for several days; even the ship's biscuit had been so spoiled by the sea water shipped in recent gales that "only the worms within it could gain nourishment therefrom".[7] Roberto and Giovanni Matteo had shared with their fellows the new wine, the chickens and the mutton that they had brought on board; now that these eatables were gone the Milanese were as hungry as the rest.

By nine o'clock that evening the ship was safely berthed. Some of her passengers went ashore; the *garbino* was blowing strongly now, but they cared little for it. Even within the harbour walls the waves were coming as great rollers; although the ship was at anchor and securely fastened she rolled so violently that no one could keep his feet on deck. At about three o'clock in the morning the look-out sighted a vessel coming swiftly in to Mello harbour. The captain could not at first identify this craft; he feared that one or more Turkish ships might be approaching. He therefore

---

* From the south-west. The west wind was called *provenza*, the *scirocco* came from the south-east.

sent a signal to ask her name and the intentions of her master. When the reply came, it was reassuring and very welcome, for the newcomer had on board the Papal Legate, Cardinal Scarampo, on his way to Rome from Rhodes. Both Sanseverino and Butigella were delighted by the news; they were, indeed, "contenti, lieti, et consolati".

Soon there was an exchange of visits. Cardinal Scarampo showed the Milanese nobles great favour and made them many gifts. He presented to Roberto various beautifully ornamented weapons and armour, including swords and shields of Turkish workmanship,[8] to add to the souvenirs Roberto had bought in Rhodes and Cairo. The Cardinal's Auditor proved to be their old friend—and late fellow-pilgrim—Antonio Capodilista. He must have set out for Rhodes very shortly after his return to Venice with the rest of the party on September 6th, unless he parted from them during the return journey when the *Loredana* put in to Rhodes for a few days. Antonio called upon Butigella aboard Francesco di Alberto's ship; they greeted one another "with the utmost warmth". The Cardinal Legate had sent the Milanese an offer to supply any provisions they might need; this they accepted with enthusiasm. In due course there arrived quantities of chickens, meat, dry wood and faggots for cooking, together with figs and melons to give variety to their diet. Sanseverino went to dine with the Cardinal in his cabin; he was astounded by the richness of the appointments. This private cabin seemed to him "more like a palace than the most beautiful house on terra firma", decked out as it was with silken hangings, the table being set with gold and silver plate. Butigella had stayed behind, feeling ill; Scarampo sent him a special gift of white bread, fresh wine, and various confections of syrup and sugar "in the hope of restoring his health and spirits".[9]

The Lieutenant of the Grand Master of Rhodes, Giovanni di Cardona, now arrived in a swift new galley to join the Legate's party. Yet another ship put in to Mello to repair the ravages caused by the storm; her *patrono* was a Venetian named Antonio Tragorino, who was carrying a cargo of salt to Venice for Andrea Cornaro, Sanseverino's host in Cyprus on the outward voyage. He too came to call, bringing with him a man-at-arms from the court of the Duchess of Milan, an old friend of Bosso and Butigella. This was Gaspare da Riva; he was able to tell the Milanese all the most recent news and gossip from their home town. The whole party had a long and lively discussion of the political implications of the death of King Alfonso of Naples;[10] Roberto must have been relieved to hear that Ferrante— supported by the Duke of Milan as well as by the new Pope*—appeared to be holding his position firmly.

Greatly cheered and encouraged by these encounters, and taking advantage of a lull in the weather, the Milanese persuaded Francesco di Alberto to continue the voyage. On Monday, November 6th, they left Mello; the days slipped quietly by as the ship tacked her way towards the coast of Istria. The winds, however, again became contrary so that on some days more was lost than was gained. Once again supplies ran low, water had to be rationed, and the passengers were allowed to make themselves only one hot meal a day. Another cloud of depression settled upon both passengers and crew. Francesco told the Milanese that he had not known "so terrible a voyage for the last thirty years".

Sanseverino and Butigella determined to get ashore, if they could, at Modone, in order to hear Mass on the feast of Santa Caterina.† They also hoped to enjoy a few good nights' rest away from their hated ship. They made harbour successfully, landing at once in order to explore the city with its splendid fortifications, before making their way to the Cathedral to inspect its relics of St. Athanasius and St.

---

* Pius II.

† November 25th. The sailors had a superstition that "it was unlucky to be at sea on St. Catherine's Day".

Leo. The Milanese had spent only three nights in this city when Francesco di Alberto sent the ship's boat to the quay with a message that as he intended to sail that evening they had better come aboard without delay.[11] Sanseverino and Butigella had to leave their beds at two in the morning; "they had much ado to induce the officials to open the city gate for them so that they could reach the harbour at this hour". In the end, however, it was not possible to leave port until Monday, December 4th, for wind and rain increased to a crescendo that frightened the *patrono* and his crew into immobility. When at last they were again at sea, calm peaceful days and warm nights—"as though the season was June or midsummer"—alternated with tempest. Driving sleet and snow left icicles hanging from the shrouds; the sailors' hands were so numbed by the cold that they fumbled when they tried to reef down the sails. The air was "full of curses and lamentable cries." . . . With one voice "they all began to cry for mercy and to invoke the Lord God, and Our Lady, beseeching first one saint and then another to intercede for them; with all the tears and devotion that they could muster."

After passing the island of Corfu the ship reached calmer seas, making some progress, but the fitful winds seemed to come always from the wrong quarter. Once again a blanket of despair settled upon the pilgrims. It appeared to Roberto that, in his customary phrase, "they were taking a thousand years" to reach Venice. In actual fact, the voyage was not abnormally prolonged. At this time of year the return trip from Jaffa to Venice might take anything up to two and a half months. Indeed, in 1506 a party of pilgrims remained at sea for nineteen weeks and a day, so that they were worn out with their "outragyous long lyenge upon the see".[12] Discipline in Francesco di Alberto's ship was poor; the crew grumbled and reviled their officers, to the great discomfort of the passengers. On one occasion, on Tuesday, December 12th, *patrono* and sailors almost came to blows.[13] Certainly this was in no way a happy ship: both passengers and crew were glad to think that they were nearing their journey's end. When the mountains of Ragusa were sighted Sanseverino was so pleased that he wrote in the *Viaggio*[14] praises of the prowess and industry of the whole ship's company, forgetting his former dissatisfaction.

This pleasure was short-lived. Soon the wind blew strongly from a contrary point: by Tuesday, December 19th, the pilgrims found that they were still three hundred miles from Venice. By the fury of the gale, and "la fortuna . . . orribilissima", they were drawn right off course; the *patrono* tried throwing out an anchor, but could not find bottom. The next day thick fog settled round them; although they were at least able to anchor the ship, they were still in great danger, suffering as well acute misery from cold and hunger. The Milanese friends determined to disembark at Ancona, in order to fulfil their vow of a pilgrimage to the shrine of Our Lady at Loreto.[15] For this purpose they needed the help of one of the ship's officers, since the *patrono* was disinclined to make this port. Roberto chose a Venetian named Jacomo Trono, together they began to make a plan. As the fog lifted the pilgrims caught occasional glimpses of distant mountains, for they were now coming closer to shore. On Christmas Day they discovered to their joy that the ship was standing off Ancona. This was the signal for unrestrained rejoicing. Many of the Sienese pilgrims combined with Sanseverino and Butigella to bribe the *patrono*—through the agency of Jacomo Trono—to set them ashore. It cost twenty-five ducats to persuade him to break his contract, but in the end the resolute pilgrims succeeded in winning his consent if not his co-operation. Trono found a Venetian trader called Baldessare Falasco, who happened to be in the port with his *barcha*. In this small boat he agreed to row ashore all who wanted to land. They had to leave their heavy baggage in Martin's charge to go on to Venice by the sea route,

but Francesco di Alberto promised—with some optimism—
that it would reach the custom house there long before they
themselves arrived in the city. Bidding farewell to the
patrono and his ship, tipping the officers and men, and each
paying a ducat to Falasco their rescuer, the pilgrims
scrambled ashore, delighted to feel solid ground beneath
their feet.

LANDFALL

> .. With the grace of God and of the most glorious
> Virgin his Mother, they left the ship and reached the
> shore . . . as though they had come out of darkness
> into light, leaving hell and returning to paradise . . .
> they felt greater pleasure, joy, contentment and
> consolation—at finding themselves on dry land—
> than ever before in their lives.
>
> Roberto da Sanseverino:
> *Viaggio in Terra Santa*, 1458

No sooner had the pilgrims stepped ashore than they found
a very well-informed Neapolitan gentleman waiting to
receive them, who could give them news of all that had come
to pass during their absence. Before leaving Acre the
pilgrims had heard of the death of Pope Calixtus III and
the election of Aeneas Sylvius Piccolomini, the Cardinal of
Siena, as his successor.[1] Apart from this one fact, and the
rather stale news of affairs in Aragon that had reached
them at Mello, the Milanese knew nothing of social or
political events. They were particularly eager for tidings
of Francesco Sforza and his doings, since these affected
them all very closely. The Neapolitan, Rosso da Diano,
showed great friendliness, particularly towards Sanseverino.
He invited them all to supper at his house, where they met
his wife and sons and spent a delightful evening, alternately
relating their own experiences and listening to all their
host had to tell them of recent happenings. After supper,
which was "copious and delicate", according to Roberto,
the pilgrims went thankfully to rest, glad indeed to be free

from the sordid quarters they had endured during their voyage.

Next morning, many gentlemen of Ancona came to call. With them was the ship's officer, Jacomo Trono, who had arranged their disembarkation, accompanied by two friends, lately passengers in Francesco's ship, who proposed to travel overland to Venice in company with the Milanese, in defiance of Francesco's prohibition. All went together to hear Mass at S. Ciriaco, on the headland overlooking sea and harbour. They then dined at Rosso's house, enjoying a meal as copious and delicate as supper had been the night before. The afternoon was spent in hiring horses and making arrangements to ride the following day to the shrine of Our Lady of Loreto in order to fulfil their vows.

About the hour of Vespers the visitors paid their respects to the civic authorities of Ancona and were shown honour in return. The *Signoria* invited Sanseverino and Butigella to help them settle a dispute between the *Comune* and the Cardinal of Pavia, who at that time was Papal Legate for the Marches of Ancona. This quarrel concerned a Genoese corsair to whom the *Comune* had given a safe-conduct; the Legate strongly objected to his protection and wished the pirate to be punished. A visit to the Cardinal, on behalf of the city fathers, meant that the Milanese would have to make a hazardous expedition across mountains and over snow-bound tracks; this they were not very willing to do, but they finally agreed to undertake the mission in order to oblige their hosts.

Roberto da Sanseverino was near his home territory, for he had been born in the Marches and his family still held lands there. Butigella had never been in Ancona before, so he was pleased by the opportunity to explore the city before they left for Loreto in the company of the Venetians and of Rosso's son Giovanni who would act as their guide. On Thursday, December 28th, everyone climbed to the shrine on the flank of the mountain where Our Lady's

House is enfolded within a massive church. After hearing Mass and making their offerings, they all continued on their way to visit the Cardinal Legate.

Like Butigella, the Cardinal Giovanni Castiglione was a native of Pavia, where his family had dwelt for many generations. He was an ambitious man who had even held some tenuous hopes of securing election to the Papacy, but he had been won by fair words to support the successful candidate, the Cardinal of Siena, in opposition to the powerful Frenchman who so nearly won the election in 1458. Castiglione was vain and easily flattered; he saw himself as a man of great influence and had no mean opinion of his own abilities. Pope Pius II afterwards said of him[2] that he "thought himself very wise and eloquent" and believed that he could do everything, even cook, better than anyone else in the whole College of Cardinals.

Since they knew his reputation for arrogance and pomposity, the Milanese were surprised as well as pleased when the Cardinal welcomed them most graciously, inviting the whole party to dinner. Butigella and Sanseverino sat at the Legate's own table, the Venetians at another in company with the Cardinal's personal friends and staff. Afterwards, Butigella presented the *Signoria's* case with some delicacy. In the end, the dispute was settled with surprisingly little discussion. Roberto has nothing to say of its outcome; his whole preoccupation is with the deep snow, the ice, and the "grandissimo freddo" with which the travellers had to contend on their journey back to Ancona.[3]

Upon their return the friends were again entertained by Rosso da Diano; as soon as possible they visited the city governors to tell them what they had been able to arrange with the Legate. The officials of the *Comune*, naturally delighted to hear that agreement had been reached, complimented Sanseverino and Butigella upon their "eloquence and tact". Neither of these qualities was conspicuous in Roberto; it was a good thing that he had left the talking to the gentler and more persuasive Giovanni Matteo, but they both shared in the diplomatic success. Next day was Sunday, the last day of the old year; the Milanese took leave of the *Signoria*, and the hospitable Rosso da Diano, departing from Ancona betimes in the morning. Two of the three Venetians went with them, while Jacomo Trono stayed on to see whether he could persuade those sailors who had deserted from Francesco di Alberto's ship to rejoin her company and help take her on to Venice. The eldest son of Rosso da Diano joined the party, for he had decided to accompany them all the way to Milan, a city that he had a great longing to see.

The last night of 1458 was spent at Sinigaglia; on New Year's Day the whole company rode to Fano where Roberto, son of Sigismondo Malatesta Lord of Rimini, had come to meet and dine with them. The same day they pressed on to Pesaro, where more celebrities came to greet them. The next two days were spent in this city, whence a full day's ride brought them to Rimini. Because Sigismondo himself was from home, another of his sons met the Milanese at the city gate. It was now Butigella's turn to make contact with his friends; he was greatly pleased when his kinsman the Marquis Carlo Pia of Carpi* came to visit him in Rimini. Since all members of this family were charming and civilized people, it was a very agreeable meeting. Next day, January 4th, the whole party attended Mass in the Church of S. Francesco, then, after dining at their inn, the travellers set out again in the company of all their friends, who rode with them for several miles.

Sanseverino believed that it would be advisable to ask for a safe-conduct through the territory of Federigo da Montefeltro of Urbino, since Federigo at this time was waging war with Sigismondo Malatesta. Roberto had no

---

* Carpi is a little town between Mantua and Modena. The Pia family, though neither rich nor politically important, had a strong influence on Renaissance culture.

mind to become a hostage; he therefore sent his servant Giov' Antonio Drella to arrange matters. Drella—now fully recovered from his sea-sickness—proved as efficient as ever. He returned, not only with the desired permission, but also with two horses apiece for Sanseverino and Butigella. Federigo da Montefeltro was a courteous person; he was at the same time a shrewd and foresighted ruler of his little mountain fastness; he quickly saw the value of establishing good relations with Francesco Sforza through showing civility to his kinsman. He might one day need Sforza's protection.

The way was easier now, the mountains lay far behind the travellers as they approached the River Savio. They took a meal at an inn near the river bank before pressing on to Ravenna, where they arrived late that night. The crossing of the Savio had delayed them considerably because the river was frozen over; they were glad to find warmth and rest at an inn in Ravenna. Next day they took things easily, travelling no more than eighteen miles. They were now passing through Este lands; before long they would reach Venetian soil. The spirits of the party rose as they looked forward to rejoining their friends within a day or two. On January 8th the party mounted their horses before dawn; they rode a good many miles by torchlight in order to reach Chioggia in time to attend Mass. Afterwards they rested and took a meal before the last stage of their journey to Venice. The horses were sent in the charge of a servant to Padua, where they would wait until needed for the ride to Milan. Other horses that had been lent to the travellers were returned to their owners in Pesaro; for the last twenty-five miles the party would have to travel by water.

This journey across the lagoon was made in a small open boat, which had to make wide detours in order to avoid the frozen fringes and shallows where the extreme cold had left miniature ice-floes very dangerous to so frail a craft. The pilgrims did not reach Venice until two hours before midnight; they were glad to go straight to the house of the Duke of Milan where, as before, arrangements had been made for them to stay. Here they were welcomed "with affection and many kisses", hearing with pleasure up-to-date news of the Duke and Duchess of Milan and of their own families.

Butigella's brother Conradino and the Seneschal of Roberto da Sanseverino should have been in Venice with the Milanese Ambassador, waiting to greet them, in answer to letters that the travellers had written from Modone. However, when he heard that they had disembarked at Ancona, Conradino Butigella assumed that the Milanese would go straight to Lombardy by way of Romagna, following the line of the Via Emilia. He had therefore left Venice three days before their arrival.[4]

After a full night's rest Sanseverino and Butigella felt sufficiently refreshed to pay their official visits, before attending Mass in S. Marco to give thanks for their safe return. The Doge and the *Signoria* showed them all the welcome and respect they felt to be their due.[5] Francesco Capodilista, the eldest brother of Gabriele, was at this time Paduan Ambassador;[6] it is to be supposed that he sent word to Gabriele, in Padua, that the travellers would soon be on their way to that city. When Mass was over Butigella and Sanseverino were free to associate with their friends and to make arrangements for the recovery of the gear they had left in Francesco di Alberto's ship. This was made unexpectedly easy for them by the arrival in Venice of their friend Jacomo Trono, who had come over from Istria (where the ship then lay) in a small boat in order to tell them that their luggage was safe in the charge of Roberto's German servant, and that the ship would reach Venice very shortly.

Many pilgrims arriving in Venice after an exhausting voyage were glad enough to stay there for some time to rest and to recover appetite and equilibrium. The Milanese Gian Giacomo Trivulzio needed twelve days' repose after his return from Palestine in 1476 for, although he was a young and active man—considerably younger than either Roberto or Gian Matteo—he found himself "tutto conquassato dal mare."[7] Even those who came overland, like Sanseverino's party, were pleased to have an excuse to linger there in peace and quiet. To await the arrival of their luggage was to these pilgrims a pleasure rather than an anxiety.

Friday, January 12th, found the Milanese friends still residing in Duke Francesco's house, while they waited for news that the horses and mules were ready for them at Padua. Word came that evening; about midnight they disposed themselves and their luggage in two boats and started for Fusina. At this point they could take their craft into the mouth of the River Brenta and thence to Padua. Beautiful gardens of villas belonging to retired business-men from Venice, and the richer citizens of Padua, stretched down to the water's edge, tranquil and inviting even at this time of the year. The travellers found an inn, perched on a bank high above the river, where they could pause for breakfast and linger in the winter sunshine. It was ten o'clock at night before they reached the city, but there at the gate to meet them was their old friend Gabriele Capodilista, with a number of others who had made the pilgrimage with them. Gabriele made much of Sanseverino and Butigella, insisting that they must be his guests. Late as it was, the same evening Gabriele's brother Francesco (the ambassador) came to call, accompanied by a crowd of Paduan gentlemen and doctors from the *Studio*.[8]

The Milanese enjoyed a stay of several days in Padua. They had arrived just in time to attend the marriage of Francesco Capodilista's daughter to Benvenuto da Treviso,* —"Notabile caualiero et gentilhomo paduano"—and to share in the wedding festivities. Francesco himself was taking a holiday from his duties in order to give his daughter

* The text gives "Tunisi", but as he is later referred to as "da Triuise", Treviso is the most likely surname.

away. On the Sunday following this wedding, Roberto and Giovanni Matteo set out to ride the eight miles to Santa Maria di Artone in order to fulfil the vow taken on board ship at the height of the storm. Many friends accompanied the party, among them the *condottiere* Lodovico Malvezzi and Roberto's kinsman Francesco da Sanseverino.* After Mass they returned by way of the baths at Abano to a beautiful villa, about three miles short of Padua, that belonged to Gabriele; here they dined in great magnificence before returning to the city.

The same day, Roberto was delighted to renew another contact. The Englishman, John Tiptoft Earl of Worcester, had rented a house in Padua while he studied there under the most famous doctors of the age. This was a very pleasant encounter, for the friends had much to say to one another. When at last they parted it was with "many affectionate embraces and much tenderness". The Milanese then returned to Gabriele's house to enjoy further his lordly hospitality. Next morning, after hearing Mass in S. Antonio and inspecting all the treasures in the sacristy, the Milanese said their farewells. Many friends[9] rode with them for two miles out of the city, but not Gabriele Capodilista, for he felt "somewhat infirm" so preferred to stay at home. Pressing gifts upon each other, and protesting their eternal friendship, the Paduans returned home, while the Milanese rode on towards Lonato, where they intended to stay the night. After this they made swift progress towards Brescia, for now they were on well-trodden roads, beyond the perilous and slippery mountain paths they had traversed for so long. Their route took them close to the houses of several acquaintances and local landowners who thought it prudent to show favour to kinsfolk of the Duke of Milan. Thus they were seldom at a loss for hospitality. Indeed, at Brescia one of the greatest nobles, Cesare da Martinengo, came to meet them, with the intention of carrying off Sanseverino and

* More likely to be Roberto's brother than his son Giovanni Francesco.

Butigella "to his house in Brescia, where he had prepared quarters for them where they might dine richly and honourably. But they had already dined at Rezzato." Nevertheless, the travellers paid a visit to the Captain of the city whom Roberto described as "molto domestico et amicho suo": he and Martinengo "with light-hearted affection and the best of good-will" did everything that they could to persuade them to stay in the city. But they were obdurate. Finally, all the chief citizens rode with them four miles upon the road, still entreating them to turn back.

By Friday, January 19th, a week after they had left Venice, Sanseverino and Butigella reached the eastern suburbs of Milan. The Duke, out on a hunting expedition when news was brought of their coming, met them near the Porta Romana. Several old friends also were there: the Marquis Lodovico Gonzaga of Mantua, Corrado da Fogliano, and a dozen others,[10] all of whom welcomed the newcomers most warmly. Afterwards, they called on the Duchess, meeting at her court many more relations and friends. Sforza's heir, Galeazzo, was away from home; Roberto was somewhat put out by what he held to be a failure in courtesy, but he left a message of greeting for Galeazzo before setting out for his own home. Although it was by then one o'clock in the morning, the whole household was at the door to greet Roberto and his friend. His wife* the Contessa Johanna, their sons, Roberto's two brothers and their wives, and a multitude of ladies and gentlemen received them with every sign of joy, extending their affectionate welcome to Butigella who had not yet had time to visit his own family.[11]

At last the greetings were completed. Giovanni Matteo was now free to make his way to his own house where he found, as he had expected, his wife and his sons, all safe and well and overjoyed to see him again. The experience had

* She was his first wife; Roberto did not marry Lucrezia Malavolti (see p. 32) until 1473.

left less mark upon Butigella than upon Roberto, who seemed to have acquired a new geniality and tolerance. He could still take umbrage and lose his temper on occasion, as he showed a few years later when he burst uninvited into the council chamber of Duke Lodovico il Moro to demand an increase in his salary.* Again, it was his headstrong character that led Roberto into the rash skirmish on the banks of the Upper Adige that caused his death.† After his pilgrimage Roberto seems to have matured, even though he was nearly forty years old when he set out on his travels. The development of his character is as clearly revealed in the *Viaggio* as that of any diarist that can readily be called to mind.

The pilgrimage had lasted no more than nine months, although it had seemed an eternity while the party lay becalmed at sea, or almost shipwrecked, nearly destroyed by the heat of the desert, or frozen on the mountains. Now, it was an experience to be described according to ability and taste, embellished perhaps with fancies and strange facts. Neverthless, this Spring Voyage, like all others, held a deep and wordless significance for those who had ventured so far with so pious an aim. The *Viaggio in Terra Santa* ends appropriately with a prayer that to all who have made such a journey may be vouchsafed "so jocund a return", a sentiment echoed by Capodilista and by William Wey, and by all the other, nameless, faceless, pilgrims who made up the expedition.

* This was largely a personal quarrel. Philip de Commynes was probably right in saying: "Two men of such character could never bear each other." *Mémoires*, ed. J. Calmette, vol. III, p. 14.

† He was drowned by the weight of his armour when he fell wounded into the river. His body was later taken to Milan and buried in the church of S. Francesco, in the chapel that he himself had built.

NAMES OF PILGRIMS IN 1458

Antonio Loredan, *patrono* of the galley *Loredana*.
Niccolò Loredan, his son.
Baldessare Diedo, his cousin, captain of the galley.

Roberto da Sanseverino, Lord of Caiazzo.
    His servants: Guiniforte (or Boniforte) Smagioso of Piacenza.
                     Giovanni Antonio Drella of Parma.
                     Martino Tedesco.

Giovanni Matteo Butigella of Pavia.
    His servants: Hilario Gentili of Tortona.
                     Giovanne Puro of Novara.

Carlo Bosso of Milan.
    His servants: Giovanni da Gliusiano ⎫ of Milan.
                     Pasquino di Mazi ⎬

Giovanni Martino de Ferrariis of Parma.
    His servant: Antonio Calistano of Parma.

Domenico da Calcenoni of Lodi.

Fenone de Eustachio of Pavia.

Gabriele Capodilista ⎫ of Padua.
Antonio Capodilista ⎬
    Their servant: Thomaso.

John Tiptoft Earl of Worcester.
    His retinue of twenty-seven servants and chaplains (including, perhaps, John Hurlegh).

William Wey, Fellow of Eton.

Anton Pelchinger, professor of Tegernsee.

Appendix A

A Dutch pilgrim who wrote a brief diary.

A pilgrim who died on the journey to Jericho; other Western pilgrims who accompanied Roberto da Sanseverino on his return from Cairo; a party of Sienese who shared his homeward voyage.

APPENDIX B

THE SIX NARRATIVES

(i) Roberto da Sanseverino: *Viaggio in Terra Santa*, 1458. Printed and edited by Gioacchino Maruffi, Bologna 1888. vol. 229 of the series edited by Giosuè Carducci; *Scelta di Curiosità Letterarie inedite o rare del secolo XIII al XVII.*

There are four manuscript versions; one is at Bologna (Biblioteca Universitaria, Cod. 1723), another (partial) version at Parma (R. Biblioteca Palatina, Cod. 800), an eighteenth-century copy in Milan* (Biblioteca Tirvulziana, Cod. N.83), and a sumptuous—perhaps not quite contemporary—manuscript that was once in the Biblioteca Silva at Cinisello and latterly in the Arconati Collection; its present whereabouts is not known.

The Bolognese MS., written within a year or two of the expedition, is the most complete and was the basis of Maruffi's edition. It is well and clearly written, in one hand throughout. There are some inaccuracies in Maruffi's transcript, e.g. '*sopra scripto*' for *illustrissimo* and '*stato*' for *restato* on the same page (c. 128ʳ). An unfortunate misreading by Maruffi converted '*osseter*' into '*esseter*' and so created a mythical 'John, Earl of Exeter', that concealed the identity of John Tiptoft Earl of Worcester for many years.

The Parma MS. is only nineteen pages long, for it contains merely a part of the journey—the expedition to Mount Sinai—but in the course of it several errors and inconsistencies are found. Some of the corrections make the text more obscure than it was before. The suggestion, made by Maruffi, that the emendations are Sanseverino's, seems to me quite unacceptable. The notes belong to a later date and were probably written well after Roberto's death.† It is possible

---

* See R. J. Mitchell: 'Una Nota al Viaggio in Terrasanta di Roberto da Sanseverino', *Archivio Storico per le provincie Parmensi*, ser. iv, vol. V (1953).

† A. Gregorini: 'Sul Codice della Bibl. Reale di Parma n. 800', in *Rassegna Bibliografica della Letteratura Italiana*, Pisa, 1897, pp. 328-9.

however, that some sentences of the Parma MS. are in Sanseverino's hand, for parts of this very uneven version of the *Viaggio* bear a considerable resemblance to the letters* that Roberto wrote in his own hand to Francesco Sforza. Other passages, notably at the top of c. 3^r., might be in the handwriting of Butigella.† It is significant that the Parma MS. is written in the first person, although the marginal annotations sometimes mention "*il autore*"; all the other versions have the third person throughout. Certainly the Parma codex is closest to the author; possibly it is a fragment of the earliest draft of the complete *Viaggio* written by Sanseverino himself or at his dictation.

* * *

(ii) Gabriele Capodilista: *Itinerario in Terra Santa*, 1458. Printed by John Vydenast at Perugia [before June 15th, 1475]. A microfilm of one of the Bologna copies has been made by kind permission of the Direttore of the Archiginnasio at Bologna, and is deposited in the Bodleian Library at Oxford.

There are six copies of the *Itinerario in Terra Santa* in Italian libraries,‡ and the *Gesamtkatalog der Wiegendrucke* (Band VI, Leipzig 1934, no. 6024) cites another example in the Biblioteca Colombina at Seville which I have not been able to examine.

The six copies are:

1 Florence: Biblioteca Nazionale, Inc. P.6.17. (Lacks Boncambio's preface.)
2 Florence: Biblioteca Riccardiana, Inc. 224.
3 Bologna: Archiginnasio $\dfrac{16}{H.VI.4}$
4 Bologna: Biblioteca Universitaria, B.IX.54.
5 Perugia: Biblioteca Augusta, Inc. 1090.
6 Venice: Biblioteca Marciana, Inc. 1206. (Lacks two folios.)

The principal MSS. of this work are: (i) the Pirelli copy (whereabouts unknown); (ii) the MS. presented to the Convent of S. Bernar-

---

* E.g. Bibliothèque Nationale, MS. Italien 1588, fo. 80^r.

† Cf. Bibliothèque Nationale, MS. Italien 1588, fo. 90^r.

‡ See *Indice Generale degli Incunaboli delle biblioteche d'Italia* compiled by T. M. Guarnaschelli and E. Valenzieri, 1948, No. 2437. Only five are named here, but there is another copy at Perugia, in the Biblioteca Augusta: Inc. 1090.

Appendix B

dino in Padua, now the property of Commendatore Astorre Mayer in Milan; (iii) one in the Biliothèque Nationale, Paris (MS. Ital. 896); and (iv) William Beckford's copy in the British Museum, Add. MS. 17481.

* * *

(iii) Giovanni Matteo Butigella: *Historia Jerosolomitana*. In the three known MS. copies of this work G. M. Butigella is cited as the author* although the main body of the work is copied from the *De redemptione & captione Terrae Sanctae* of Jacques de Vitry.

The three MSS. are:

1 Florence: Biblioteca Laurenziana, Cod. Plut. 89 infra 18.
2 Milan: Biblioteca Ambrosiana, Cod. T.102 supr.
3 Philadelphia: Free Library; J. F. Lewis Collection of European MSS., etc., No. 138.

The two last were both written by the scribe Johannes de Camenago, in 1463 and 1459 respectively.

The Ambrosiana copy has a slightly fuller version of the preface than that given in the Laurenziana MS. It is a pretty book; it has a good border on fo. 1. with *putti* playing musical instruments and supporting a shield whose charge is no longer decipherable. The initial C is foliated on a gold ground, with coloured interlacing strapwork. The capitals at the beginning of the chapters throughout the book are of excellent proportions and lightly flourished with lilac, red or blue. At the end an eighteenth-century hand has written some extracts copied from the Trivulziana version of Sanseverino's *Viaggio*: this unknown writer is also aware of the Cinisello MS. of the *Viaggio* for he quotes a short passage from it.†

* * *

(iv) Anton Pelchinger: a conventional description of the Holy Places in and about Jerusalem that contains no personal or topical comments. As far as is known, the copy (No. 3012) in the Dept. of MSS. in the Österreichische Nationalbibliothek, Vienna, is unique; although Dr.

* Cf. C. Mazzuchelli: *Scrittori d'Italia*, Brescia 1753, p. 2472. But see A. M. Bandini; *Cat. Cod. Lat. Bibl. Mediceae Laurentianae*, Firenze 1776, tom. III.

† I am most grateful to dott. Caterina Santoro, Direttrice of the Biblioteca Trivulziana, for calling my attention to these notes.

Franz Unterkircher tells me there may be another at Munich, I have not succeeded in tracing it.

*   *   *

(v) An anonymous Dutch pilgrim wrote a fragmentary account of the Holy Places, contained in a MS. in the British Museum. Add. MS. 10286, pp. 137-46.

*   *   *

(vi) William Wey: *Itineraries* (Bodleian Library, Oxford). MS. Bodley 264, ed. G. Williams for the Roxburghe Club, 1857; a second volume contains the map (from MS. Bodley 765) that has generally been attributed to him.

Wey's general remarks are very close indeed to *Information for Pilgrims unto the Holy Land*, printed by Wynkyn de Worde, Westminster, *c.* 1498.* This was perhaps the work of 'Master Larkes' (see R. J. Mitchell: 'Robert Langton's Pylgrymage', in *The Library*, June 1954); it was certainly written after Wey's *Itineraries*. We may well accept the editor's guess that the *Information* was written in 1481, 1487, or 1492. (See also Chapter I, pp. 19-20.)

* A facsimile was published by E. Gordon Duff, London 1893.

SELECT BIBLIOGRAPHY

[See Appendix B for bibliographical details of MSS. and printed versions of Roberto da Sanseverino's *Viaggio*, Capodilista's *Itinerario*, etc.]

MANUSCRIPTS

BOLOGNA, Bibl. Universitaria: Cod. 1723.

FLORENCE, Biblioteca Laurenziana: Cod. Ashburnham 1117.

Cod. Plut. 89 infra 18.

LONDON, British Museum: MS. Egerton 1900. (Gabriel Muffel's *Pilgrim Book*. An Italian version with wood-cuts was printed at Bologna in 1500.)

MS. Egerton Add. 1901.

Add. MS. 17481.

MILAN, Bibl. Ambrosiana: Cod. T.102 Supr.

Biblioteca Trivulziana: Cod. N.78, N.83.

OXFORD, Bodleian Library: MS. Eng. Hist. C. 381-4.

(F. Grierson's trans. of the *Commentarii* of Aeneas Sylvius Piccolomini.)

MS. Bodley 80.

MS. Canonici Misc. 127

PARIS, Bibliothèque Nationale: MS. lat. 6980.

MS. 8130.

MSS. Italien 896; 1587; 1588; 1594. (The letters of R. da Sanseverino and Butigella are in Cod. 1588.)

PARMA, R. Bibl. Palatina: Cod. Parm. 800.

PHILADELPHIA: Free Library: J. F. Lewis Collection, no. 138.*

SIENA, Archivio di Stato: Carte Particolari Famiglia Sanseverino.

Delib. del Concistoro 638.

VENICE, Archivio di Stato: Senato Mar. Registro I, II, VI.

Senato Mist. Reg. IX, X.

Sezione Notarile Testamenti B.1229.

* I have not been able to inspect this MS. personally, but the Librarian has kindly sent me a description.

Select Bibliography

PILGRIMS' ITINERARIES (PRINTED)

[Other than those in Appendix B. Full lists of pilgrims' travel books will be found in the works of Röhricht and Tobler (the latter should be used with care). This is a selection of the more interesting and relevant.]

ANGLURE, Seigneur d': *Le Saint Voyage*, ed. H. F. Bonnardot and A. Longnon, Paris, 1878.

BRASCA, Santo: *Viaggio alla sanctissima città di Ierusalem*, Milan, 1481.

BROCQUIÈRE, Bertrand de la: 'Travels', in *Early Travels in Palestine*, trans. and ed. T. Wright, London, 1848.

CASOLA, Canon Pietro: *Pilgrimage*, trans. and ed. M. M. Newett, Manchester, 1907.

CASTIGLIONE, Girolamo: *Fiore di Terra Santa*, Messina, 1499.

EHINGEN, Jörg von: *Diary*, trans. and ed. M. Letts, Oxford, 1929.

FABRI, Felix: *Wanderings*, trans. and ed. Aubrey Stewart for the Palestine Pilgrims Text Society, 1892.

GUYLFORDE, Sir Richard: *Pylgrymage*, ed. Sir. H. Ellis (Camden Society), London, 1851.

IBN BATÚTA, *Travels in Asia and Africa*, trans. H. A. R. Gibb, London, 1929.

Information for Pilgrims unto the Holy Land, ed. E. Gordon Duff, London, 1893.

KEMPE, Margery: *The Book of Margery Kempe*, ed. W. Butler Bowden, London, 1936.

PILOTI, Emmanuele: *Traité . . . sur le passage en Terre Sainte*, ed. Pierre-Herman Dopp, Louvain/Paris, 1958.

POGGIBONSI, Niccolò da: *Libro d'Oltramare*, ed. A. Bacchi della Lega, Bologna, 1881. 2 vols.

POLONER, John: *Description of the Holy Land*, trans. and ed. A. Stewart for the Palestine Pilgrims Text Society, London, 1894.

SIENA, Mariano da: *Viaggio in Terra Santa*, 1431. Parma, 1863.

SUCHEM, Ludolph von: *Travels*, trans. and ed. A. Stewart for the Palestine Pilgrims Text Society, London, 1895.

SYMON, Semeonis: *Itinerarius*, ed. Mario Esposito, Dublin, 1960.

TAFUR, Pero: *Travels and Adventures*, trans. and ed. M. Letts, London, 1926.

TORKINGTON, Sir Richard: *Diary*, ed. W. J. Loftie, London, 1884.

Select Bibliography

TRIVULZIO, Gian. Giacomo: *G.G.T. in Terra Santa*, 1476, by E. Motta, *Arch. Storico Lombardo*, ser. ii, vol. III, Milan, 1866.

Visits to the Holy Places . . . in 1384, by Leonardo Frescobaldi, Giorgio Gucci, and Simone Sigoli, trans. from the Italian by Fr. Theophilus Bellorini and Fr. Eugene Hoade. Jerusalem 1948. (Publications of the Studium Biblicum Franciscanum, No. 6.) See also: Simone Sigoli; *Viaggio al Monte Sinai*, Naples 1855.

REFERENCE BOOKS AND ARTICLES

ALLEN, P. S.: *The Age of Erasmus*, Oxford, 1914.

AMAT DI SAN FILIPPO, Pietro: *Gli illustri viaggiatori italiani con una antologia dei loro scritti*, Rome, 1885.

ATIYA, A. S.: *The Crusade in the Later Middle Ages*, London, 1938.

BEER, E. S. de: 'The Development of the Guide-book until the early XIX Century', *Journal of the Brit. Arch. Assoc.*, ser. iii, vol. XV (1952).

BEER, Sir Gavin de: *Early Travellers in the Alps*, London, 1930.

BELABRE, Baron de: *Rhodes of the Knights*, Oxford, 1908.

BENZONI, Antonio: 'Un carme inedite di Laura Brenzoni in onore di Roberto da Sanseverino', *Archivio Veneto*, ser. iv, vol. XXXIV (1939).

CARLI, Enzo: *Catalago-Mostra delle Tavolette di Biccherna* ecc. Florence, 1950.

Cronaca di Anonimo Veronese, 1448-1488, ed. G. Soranza, Venice, 1915.

FERRARI, H. M. de Grado: *Une chaire de médecine au XVe siècle*, Paris, 1899.

FRATI, L.: 'Notizie Biografiche di G. B. Refrigerio', *Giornale storico*, XII, fasc. 36.

GIUSTINIANI, B.: *Historia di tutti gli Ordini Militari e Caualliereschi*, Venice, 1692.

GOLUBOVICH, P. Girolamo, O.F.M.: *Biblioteca bio-bibliografica della Terra Santa e dell' oriente Francescano*, Florence 1923. (This splendid work only goes up to 1345.)

Handbook of Oriental History, Royal Historical Society, 1951.

HEYD, W.: *Histoire du commerce du Levant au moyen-âge* (French version), Leipzig, 1886.

Select Bibliography

HILL, Sir George: *History of Cyprus*, Cambridge. 3 vols. 1940-8.

Indice Generale degli Incunaboli delle biblioteche d'Italia, per cura di T. M. Guarnaschelli and E. Valenzieri, Rome, 1948.

LANE, F. C.: *Venetian ships and ship-builders of the Renaissance*, Baltimore, 1934.

MAS LATRIE, Louis de: *Histoire de L'île de Chypre sous le règne des princes de Lusignan*, Paris, 1861-2. 3 vols.

MAZZUCHELLI, C.: *Scrittori d'Italia*, Brescia, 1753.

MERCIER, L.: *La chasse et les sports chez les Arabes*, Paris, 1927.

MITCHELL, R. J.: *John Tiptoft*, London, 1938.

—— 'Una nota al Viaggio . . . di R. da Sanseverino,' in *Archivio Storico per le provincie Parmensi*, ser. iv, vol. V (1953).

—— 'Robert Langton's "Pylgrymage",' in *The Library*, June 1954.

—— 'Giovanni Martino da Parma: Garbazza o de Ferrariis?' *Aurea Parma*, 1958.

—— 'Antonio Loredan and the Jaffa Voyage,' in *Italian Studies*, vol. XIII (1958).

—— 'Archbishop Blackader in Venice,' in *Bollettino dell' Istituto di storia della Società e dello stato Veneziano* (Fondazione Giorgio Cini), tom I (1959).

—— 'Gabriele Capodilista,' in *Bollettino del Museo Civico di Padova*, 1960, numero 2.

—— *The Laurels and the Tiara*, London, 1962.

MOTTA, Emilio: 'Musici alla corte degli sforza,' *Arch. Storico Lombardo*, ser. i, vol. XIV (1887).

MUIR, Sir William: *The Mameluke or Slave Dynasty of Egypt, 1260-1517*, London, 1896.

'Ordine dell' Esercito ducale sforzesco, 1472-4,' *Arch. Storico Lombardo*, ser. i, vol. III (1878).

PARKS, G. B.: *The English Traveller in Italy*, vol. I, Rome, 1954.

PELLEGRIN, Elisabeth: *La Bibliothèque des Visconti et des Sforza Ducs de Milan au XVᵉ siècle*, Paris, 1955.

—— *Bibliothèque d'Humanisme et Renaissance*, tom XVII, Geneva, 1955.

PICCOLOMINI, Aeneas Sylvius: *Commentarii*, Frankfurt 1614. (See also under MSS.)

—— *Lettera a Maometto*, Naples 1952.

PRESCOTT, H. F. M.: *Jerusalem Journey*, London, 1954.

—— *Once to Sinai*, London, 1957.

RAMUSIO, Paolo: Italian trans. of Roberto Valturio, *De Re Militari*, Verona, 1483.

RÖHRICHT, R.: *Bibliotheca Geographica Palaestinae*, Berlin, 1890.
—— *Deutsche Pilgerreisen, etc.*, Innsbruck, 1900.

RUSSELL, Dorothea: *Medieval Cairo*, London, 1962.

SANGIORGIO, G.: *I Lombardi Viaggiatori fuor d'Europa*, Milan, 1882.

SIMONETTA, Cicco: 'Diarii parte ii,' in *Arch. Storico Lombardo*, ser. viii, vol. VI (1957).

SOUTHERN, R. W.: *Western Views of Islam in the Middle Ages*, Cambridge, Mass., 1962.

Stations of Rome, ed. F. J. Furnivall, Early Eng. Text Society, 1867.

STRETTON, G.: 'Aspects of Medieval Travel,' *Trans. of the R. Hist. Society*, ser. iv, vol. VII (1924).

TOBLER, Titus: *Bibliographica geographica Palestinae*, Leipzig, 1867.
—— *Descriptiones Terrae Sanctae ex saeculo VIII, IX, XII et XV*, Leipzig, 1874.

TYLER, J. E.: *The Alpine Passes*, Oxford, 1930.

VEDOVA, G.: *Biografica dei Scrittori Padovani*, Padua, 1831.

VERMIGLIOLI, G. B.: *Principi della stampa in Perugia*, Perugia, 1820.

YULE, Sir H.: *Cathay and the Way Thither*, new edn. H. Cordier, London, 1913 (Hakluyt Society), 2 vols.

ZACCARIA, V.: 'L'Epistolario di Pier Candido Decembrio,' in *Rinascimento, III* (1950).

ZANIBONI, E.: *Alberghi Italiani XIII-XVIII sec.*, Naples, 1921.

NOTES

CHAPTER ONE

(1) One such will (made by a Scottish archbishop) still exists in the Arch. di Stato at Venice, Sezione Notarile Testamenti, B.1229, Protocollo I. n. 145, cc. 121^v-122^v.

(2) *The Book of Margery Kempe*, ed. Butler Bowden, London, 1936, p. 63.

(3) Santo Brasca. He went to Jerusalem in 1480; his book, *Viaggio alla Sanctissima città di Ierusalem*, was published the following year, Milan, 1481. It is very rare, but there is a copy in the British Museum (I.A.26460). See esp. pp. 48^v-49^v, where he gives instructions to prospective pilgrims.

(4) British Museum, MS. Egerton Add. 1901.

(5) This was Girolamo Castiglione; *Fiore di Terra Santa* (third edition), Messina, 1499

(6) The *Information* was reprinted in fascimile from the first edition (Wynkyn de Worde, 1498), by E. Gordon Duff; London, 1893.

On 'Master Larkes' see R. J. Mitchell: 'Robert Langton's "Plygrimage",' in *The Library*, June 1954.

(7) *The Itineraries of William Wey*, ed. G. Williams for the Roxburghe Club, London, 1857.

(8) MS. Bodley—765.

(9) Castiglione in *Fiore di Terra Santa*, also Casola (see Bibliography) and others.

(10) R. J. Mitchell: *The Laurel and the Tiara*, London, 1962, p. 113.

(11) On July 12th, 1453. *Pii II Opera*, Basel, 1571, Ep. 162.

(12) Book VI, where an admirable account of the whole situation is given.

(13) Roberto's letters from Venice and Rhodes (May 11th and June 11th, 1458) are in the Bibliothèque Nationale, Paris. MS. 1588, fo. 65, 80.

Sforza's instructions to him are also to be found there, in MS. 1587, fo. 63-4.

Notes

(14) *Travels and Adventures of Pero Tafur*, trans. M. Letts, London, 1926, p. 55.

(15) Quoted by H. F. M. Prescott: *Jersualem Journey*, London, 1954, p. 84.

(16) A. S. Atiya: *The Crusade in the Later Middle Ages*, London, 1938, pp. 186 ff.

(17) R. S. Southern: *Western Views of Islam in the Middle Ages*, Cambridge, Mass., 1962, p. 93. The idea was first put forward by John of Segovia, d. 1485.

(18) Professor Southern quotes from Nicholas' letter to John of Segovia; see R. Klibansky and H. Bascour: 'Nicolai de Cusa De Pace Fidei', in *Med. and Ren. Studies*, III, Supplement 1956, p. 97.

(19) Pio II: *Lettera a Maometto II*, Naples, 1952. It was probably written in 1460. See Mitchell: *The Laurels, etc.*, p. 173.

(20) *Western Views of Islam etc.* p. 99.

(21) *Itinerarium Symonis Semeonis ab Hybernia ad Terram Sanctam*, ed. Mario Esposito, Dublin 1960, cap. 54.

CHAPTER TWO

(1) ed. G. Maruffi, Bologna, 1888, pp. 7-8.

(2) 'Ordine dell' Esercito ducale sforzescho, 1472-4,' *Archivi Storico Lombardo*, ser. i, vol. III (1878), p. 453.

(3) In the State Archives of Siena (Carte Particolari Famiglia Sanseverino) especially a letter dated October 12th, 1471, from one Scipio, captain of a band of horse.

(4) Printed by Antonio Benzoni: 'Un carme inedite di Laura Brenzoni in onore di R. da Sanseverino', in *Archivio Veneto*, ser. v, vol. XXIV (1939), pp. 187 ff.

(5) Giovanni Battista Refrigerio, who wrote a poem—*Il Trionfo*—in which he forecast that in Paradise Roberto would be found in the company of the two Scipios, Charlemagne, Constantine, and Belisarius. This was printed in 1487 in a pamphlet of which there is only one known copy—in the Bibl. Marciana at Venice.

(6) For instance: Paolo Ramusio's Italian translation of the *De Re Militari* written by Roberto Valturio, printed at Verona in 1483. Also Lodovico Petroni's *La Guerra dei Goti*, translated from Leonardo Bruni's *De bello italico versus Gothos*, Foligno 1470.

There is a MS. copy (Cod. N. 78) of Petroni's work in the Bibl. Trivulziana at Milan—perhaps the actual dedicatory copy.

(7) E. Motta: 'Musici alla corte degli Sforza', in *Archivio Storico Lombardo*, ser. i, vol. XIV (1887), pp. 113-40.

(8) *Ibid.*, p. 9. His name was Isaac Argiropulo.

(9) G. Maruffi, in his introduction to the *Viaggio in Terra Santa*, Bologna, 1888, p. iv.

(10) See R. J. Mitchell: 'Giovanni Martino da Parma: Garbazza o de Ferrariis?' in *Aurea Parma*, Jan.-March 1958. See also H. M. Ferrari de Grado: *Une Chaire de Médecine au XVe siècle, un professeur à l'université de Pavia . . . 1432-1472*, Paris, 1899.

(11) A manuscript at Parma, in the R. Biblioteca Palatina, Cod. 800. See R. J. Mitchell: 'Una nota al Viaggio di R. da Sanseverino,' in *Archivio Storico per le provincie Parmensi*, ser. iv, vol. V (1953).

(12) There are two MSS. of this version, one in Paris (Bibl. Nat. MS. Cat. 6980), the other in Florence (Bibl. Laurenziana, MS. Ashburnham 1117). Another version (Oxford, Bodleian, MS. Canonici Misc. 127) is dedicated to Lodovico Gonzaga.

(13) Caterina Santoro: *Gli Uffici del Domineo Sforzesco 1450-1500*, Milan, 1948, p. 675.

(14) Poems of Giovanni Battista Bosso, in Paris, Bibl. Nat. MS. Lat. 8407. See E. Pellegrin: *La Bibliothèque des Visconti e des Sforza Ducs de Milan au XVe siècle*, Paris, 1955, p. 333.

(15) See V. Zaccaria: 'L'Epistolario di P. C. Decembrio', in *Rinascimento*, III, 1 (1952), p. 112.

Also R. Sabbadini: *Classici e Umanisti da Codici Ambrosiana*. Florence 1933, p. 94.

(16) For a full description of all his MSS. (except the Bodleian MS. d'Orville 517) see Dr. Elisabeth Pellegrin, in *Bibliothèque d'Humanisme et Renaissance*, tom. XVII, Geneva, 1955, pp. 229-35.

(17) Paris, Bibliothèque Nationale, MS. Ital. 1594, pp. 131, 202.

(18) *Viaggio* p. 8.

(19) *Ibid.*, p. 15.

(20) The Codice Capodilista, in the Biblioteca del Museo Civico di Padova. MS. B.P.954, fo. 33.

(21) R. J. Mitchell: 'Gabriele Capodilista', in *Bollettino del Museo*

Notes

Civico di Padova, no. 2 (1960). They were not, as stated by A. Codazzi in his *Viaggiotori, etc.*, (see Bibliography) brothers. On the Capodilista family, see G. Vedova; *Biografica dei Scrittori Padovani*, Padua, 1831.

(22) *Ibid.*

(23) *Itinerario in Terra Santa*, Perugia [1475] p. 61.

(24) *Ibid.*, p. 70.

(25) *Ibid.*, pp. 49-50.

(26) *Ibid.*, p. 43. "dicta eclesia e molto bella & magnifica & simigliasse molto a la chesia [*sic*] de santo Antonio nostra de padoa. El choro a uno andito intorno chel circunda cum alchune capelle come e in predicta chesia [*sic*] di santo Antonio da padoa, & a santo Francesco in bologna. El sepulchro del nostro signore e denanti dal coro in mezo la chiesia come periane la predicta chiesia di sancto Antonio. . . ."

(27) Vespasiano da Bisticci, the Florentine bookseller. See *Vite di Uomini illustri del secolo XV*, ed. P. d'Ancona and E. Aeschlimann, Milan, 1951, p. 226.

(28) John Rous of Warwick, who records the conversation in his *Historia Regum Angliae*, ed. T. Hearne, Oxford, 1716, p. 5.

(29) R. J. Mitchell: *John Tiptoft*, London, 1938, pp. 23-7.

(30) *Calendar of State Papers and MSS. in Milan*, ed. A. B. Hinds, vol. I, p. 58.

(31) Thomas Fuller: *Worthies of England*, London, 1662, p. 155.

(32) John Free, in a letter addressed to his patron. Bodleian Library, Oxford, MS. Bodley 80, p. 7.

(33) Mitchell: *John Tiptoft*, pp. 188-9.

(34) August 11th, 1457. The original document is in the archives of Eton College; it was printed by the editor, G. Williams, in his introduction to *The Itineraries of William Wey* (Roxburghe Club, 1857).

CHAPTER THREE

(1) *Early Travels in Palestine*, ed. T. Wright, London, 1848, p. 284.

(2) R. Röhricht: *Deutsche Pilgerreisen, etc.*, Innsbruck, 1900 (preface).

(3) E. Zaniboni: *Alberghi Italiani* (XIII-XVIII Century), Naples, 1921, p. 65.

Notes

(4) Canon Pietro Casola. See his *Pilgrimage*, trans. M. M. Newett, Manchester, 1907, p. 130.

(5) Aeneas Sylvius Piccolomini: *Commentarii*, Book III. The translation is Flora Grierson's, Bodleian Library, Oxford, MS, Eng. Hist. C.381.

(6) The Spaniard, Pero Tafur. See his *Travels and Adventures*, trans. M. Letts, London, 1926, p. 170.

(7) A. S. Piccolomini: *Commentarii*, Book III.

(8) "De diuersi paiesi de vitramonte", *Viaggio*, p. 16.

(9) Marino Sanuto, *Diarii* (tom. VIII, ed. R. Fulin, Venice 1882, p. 472), describes the ceremony fifty years later, when a Scottish archbishop was the principal guest of honour. See R. J. Mitchell: 'Archbishop Blackader in Venice,' in *Bollettino dell' Istituto di Storia della Società e dello stato Veneziano*, Fondazione Giorgio Cini, Venice, 1959, p. 173.

(10) The text has been printed by R. J. Mitchell: 'Antonio Loredan and the Jaffa voyage,' in *Italian Studies*, XIII (1958), p. 85 (Appendix A). The contract is dated May 14th, 1458.

CHAPTER FOUR

(1) F. C. Lane: *Venetian Ships and Shipbuilders of the Renaissance*, Baltimore, 1934, chapter 1.

(2) Antonio's father was Ser Daniele Loredan, his uncle Ser Bartolomeo. The earlier galley was built in 1439. Venice, State Archives, Senato Miste, Reg. LX, c. 150 (June 8th, 1439).

(3) By an ordinance of 17th May, 1446. State Archives, Senato Mar. Registro II, c. 143.

(4) *Itinerario in Terra Santa*, p. 73.

(5) G. Stretton: 'Aspects of Medieval Travel', *Trans. of the R. Hist. Soc.*, ser. iv, vol. VII (1924), p. 84.

(6) *Itinerario*, pp. 7-8.

(7) *Itineraries of William Wey*.

(8) See Appendix B.

(9) *Die Peregrinatio van Jherusalem*, Brit. Mus. MS. Add. 10286, pp. 137-46.

(10) *The Stations of Rome*, ed. F. J. Furnivall, E. E. T. Soc., 1867, p. 37.

(11) *Viaggio*, p. 25.

Notes

(12) H. F. M. Prescott: *Jersualem Journey*, London, 1954, p. 94. Santo Brasca (*op. cit.*) also mentions this practice.

(13) *Viaggio*, p. 33.

(14) *Ibid.*, p. 37; *Itinerario*, p. 11.

(15) The letter is printed in *Archaeologia*, vol. XXXI.

(16) *Itinerario*, p. 26.

(17) *Ibid.*, p. 30.

CHAPTER FIVE

(1) Where he was visited by Pope Pius II a few years later. See Mitchell, *The Laurels and the Tiara*, p. 223.

(2) He was a Neapolitan, Don Sergio di Scripandi. *Viaggio*, p. 54.

(3) Baron de Belabre: *Rhodes of the Knights*, Oxford, 1908, p. 129. The Knights of St. John had conquered the island in 1309; in 1312 they were awarded the estates of the Knights Templar.

(4) *Viaggio*, p. 57.

CHAPTER SIX

(1) Trans. and ed. Malcolm Letts, London, 1926, p. 64.

(2) *Viaggio*, p. 62.

(3) Andrea's niece, Caterina, afterwards became Queen of Cyprus (in 1472); on the death of her husband she ruled for another sixteen years; she was then compelled to flee to Venice. She died in 1510.

(4) *Canon Pietro Casola's Pilgrimage*, p. 216.

(5) Helena Palaeologus, daughter of the Despot of the Morea. The child, Charlotte of Lusignan, succeeded her father later in the year. See p. 120.

(6) *Itinerario*, p. 37.

(7) Robert Blackader, Archbishop of Glasgow. See R. J. Mitchell: 'Archbishop Blackader in Venice,' *Bollettino dell' Istituto di storia della società e dello stato Veneziano* (Fondazione Giorgio Cini) tom I (1959), pp. 169-78.

(8) *Viaggio*, p. 67.

(9) *Ibid.*, pp. 69-70.

(10) *Itinerario*, p. 43.

Notes

(11) Friar Felix Fabri. See H. F. M. Prescott: *Jerusalem Journey*, p. 109.

(12) *Itineraries of William Wey*, introduction, p. xxviii.

CHAPTER SEVEN

(1) *Viaggio*, p. 75.

(2) P. S. Allen: *The Age of Erasmus*, Oxford, 1914, p. 235.

(3) *Viaggio*, pp. 76, 77.

(4) *Ibid.*, p. 79.

(5) *Itinerario in Terra Santa*, p. 53.

(6) *Itinerario*, p. 69.

(7) *Ibid.*, p. 55.

(8) *Pylgrymage of Sir Richard Guylforde*, pp. 29-30.

(9) *Travels and Adventures of Pero Tafur*, pp. 61-2.

(10) *Canon Pietro Casola's Pilgrimage*, p. 276.

(11) *Itinerario*, p. 43. For his description of the church, see note 26 to chapter 2.

(12) See Mitchell: 'Gabriele Capodilista,' in *Bolletino del Museo Civico di Padova*, 1960, no. 2.

CHAPTER EIGHT

(1) *The Wanderings of Felix Fabri*, trans. A. Stewart for the Pal. Pilgrims Text Soc., 1892-5, Bk. VII, pp. 283-4.

(2) *The Book of Margery Kempe*, ed. W. Butler Bowden, London, 1936, p. 70.

(3) See p. 99. For a description of this MS. see *Libri Insigni XIV-XVI secole*, Libreria Antiquaria Hoepli, Milan, 1940, p. 4.

(4) *Canon Pietro Casola's Pilgrimage*, pp. 230, 261.

(5) *Itinerarium Symonis Semeonis ab Hybernia ad Terram Sanctam*, ed. Mario Esposito, Dublin, 1960, cap. 96. This tradition is recorded by Capodilista but not by Roberto da Sanseverino.

(6) *Ibid.*, p. 107, n. 1.

(7) *Ibid.*, cap. 98.

(8) *Viaggio*, p. 81.

(9) *Ibid.*, p. 91.

(10) *Calendar of Papal Registers*, vol. XII, ed. J. A. Twemlow, London, 1933, p. 539.

Notes

(11) At University College, Oxford.

(12) London, Somerset House, P.C.C. 29, Godyn.

(13) *Viaggio*, p. 101.

(14) *Ibid.*, p. 105.

(15) B. Giustiniani gives a full description of the ceremony of knight-hood in his *Historia di tutti gli Ordini Militari e Cauallereschi*, Venice, 1692, chapter iii, pp. 43-5.

(16) Mitchell: *John Tiptoft*, pp. 101-3.

(17) *Viaggio*, p. 106.

CHAPTER NINE

(1) *Viaggio in Terra Santa*, p. 104.

(2) Paris, Bibliothèque Nationale, MS. Italien 1588, fo. 90.

(3) *Canon Pietro Casola's Pilgrimage*, p. 262.

(4) *Itineraries of William Wey*, p. 73.

(5) *Itinerario in Terra Santa*, p. 47.

(6) Mitchell: 'Gabriele Capodilista,' in *Bollettino del Museo Civico di Padova* (1960), no. 2.

CHAPTER TEN

(1) Grace Stretton: 'Some Aspects of Medieval Travel,' *Trans. of the R. Hist. Soc.*, 1924, p. 85-6.

(2) On July 26th, 1458. See Sir George Hill: *History of Cyprus*, vol. III, p. 546.

(3) *Travels and Adventures of Pero Tafur*, pp. 104-5.

(4) *Itinerario*, p. 39.

(5) In 1453. See above, pp. 21-2.

(6) Mitchell: *John Tiptoft*, pp. 47, 132.

(7) E. Motta: 'Gian Giacomo Trivulzio in Terra Santa, 1476,' *Archivio Storico Lombardo*, ser. ii, vol. III, Milan, 1866.

(8) This MS. is now in a private collection in Milan. For a full description see *Libri Insigni*, Hoepli, Milan, 1940, p. 4.

(9) Mitchell: 'Gabriele Capodilista,' in *Bollettino del Museo Civico di Padova* (1960), no. 2.

(10) As reported by Lodovico Carbone. See R. Weiss, in *Rinascimento*, no. 2 (1957), pp. 209-12.

(11) G. B. Parks; *The English Traveller in Italy*, vol. I, Rome, 1954, p. 520.

CHAPTER ELEVEN

(1) Pp. 164, 166-7.
(2) Archivio di Stato, Venice. Senato Mist. Reg. IX, c. 268.^{v}; Senato Mar, I, c. 36^r.
(3) Senato Mist. Reg. IX, c. 212.
(4) Mitchell: 'Antonio Loredan and the Jaffa Voyage,' in *Italian Studies*, vol. XIII (1958), p. 84.
(5) Bertrand de la Brocquière: *Early Travels in Palestine*, p. 294.
(6) W. Heyd: *Histoire du commerce du Levant au moyen-âge*, French edn. by Furey Raynaud, Leipzig, 1923, vol. II, pp. 464-5.
(7) Sanseverino: *Viaggio*, p. 180.
(8) No specific sum is named in the indictment. Arch. di Stato, Venice, Senato Mar, VI, c. 96^v. It is printed in Appendix B to Mitchell's 'Antonio Loredan and the Jaffa Voyage,' pp. 85-7.
(9) The series entitled 'Senato Mist. Reg. IX' and 'X', Archivio di Stato, Venice.
(10) L. Frati: 'Notizie Biografiche di Giovanni Battista Refrigerio,' *Giornale Storico*, XII, fasc. 36, no. ii, p. 335.

CHAPTER TWELVE

(1) Translated and edited by Malcolm Letts, London, 1926, p. 81.
(2) In 1446. Decembrio's covering letter has been printed by R. Sabbadini: *Classici e Umanisti dri Codici Ambrosiana*, Florence, 1933, p. 94.
(3) *Viaggio*, p. 118.
(4) *Ibid.*, p. 119.
(5) H. F. M. Prescott: *Once to Sinai*, London, 1957, pp. 23-4.
(6) *Travels and Adventures of Pero Tafur*.
(7) *Early Travels in Palestine* p. 289.
(8) *Viaggio*, p. 120.
(9) Milan, Biblioteca Ambrosiana, Cod. T.102. Supr.
(10) Ibid., c. 1^v.
(11) *Viaggio*, p. 120.
(12) *Ibid.*, p. 111.

(13) *Ibid.*, p. 123.

(14) *Ibid.*, p. 124.

(15) Quoted by Prescott: *Once to Sinai*, p. 54.

(16) *Viaggio*, p. 125.

(17) Felix Fabri's route in 1483 has been well worked out by G. W. Murray in *Geographical Journal* vol. CCXXII, part iii, Sept. 1956, pp. 335-42. Sanseverino's, however, is not susceptible to such careful plotting, since he himself was often doubtful concerning his exact whereabouts.

(18) *Viaggio*, p. 129.

(19) *Ibid.*, p. 130.

(20) Simone Sigoli: *op. cit.*, p. 57.

CHAPTER THIRTEEN

(1) *Viaggio*, p. 134.

(2) MS. Egerton 1900, fo. 123^v.

(3) *Viaggio*, p. 135.

(4) *Canon Pietro Casola's Pilgrimage*, p. 202.

(5) *Viaggio*, p. 134.

(6) Felix Fabri; quoted by Prescott, *Once to Sinai*, p. 81.

(7) *Viaggio* p. 139.

(8) *Ibid.*, p. 140. For a description of the plant see Prescott: *Once to Sinai*, pp. 115-23.

(9) *Viaggio*, p. 150.

CHAPTER FOURTEEN

(1) *Viaggio*, p. 140.

(2) *Ibid.*, p. 147. A German traveller, Ludolph von Suchem, in 1350 said that Cairo was seven times as large as Paris. *Travels*, trans. A. Stewart, London, 1895, p. 67.

(3) Ibn Batúta; *Travels in Asia and Africa*, 1325-1354, trans. H. A. R. Gibb, London, 1929, p. 50.

(4) Dorothea Russell: *Medieval Cairo*, London, 1962, pp. 26, 270-1.

(5) Quoted by Prescott: *Once to Sinai*, p. 159.

(6) *Viaggio*, p. 154.

(7) The 'Second Dynasty', i.e. the Abbasīd Khalifs. See Russell: *Medieval Cairo*, p. 34.

(8) *Viaggio*, p. 143.

(9) *Ibid.*, p. 144.

(10) *Itinerarium Symonis Semeonis ab Hybernia ad Terram Sanctam*, pp. 84, 85.

(11) *Viaggio*, p. 145.

(12) Russell: *Medieval Cairo*, pp. 31, 195-7.

(13) *Ibid.*

(14) *Itinerarium Symonis Semeonis*, p. 77.

(15) *Ibid.*, pp. 76-7.

(16) *Viaggio*, p. 153.

(17) *Visits to the Holy Places*, p. 101.

(18) *Viaggio*, pp. 154-5.

(19) *Itinerarium Symonis Semeonis*, p. 101.

(20) *Viaggio*, p. 156.

(21) *Ibid.*, p. 159.

(22) *Ibid.*, pp. 160-1.

(23) *Ibid.*, p. 163.

CHAPTER FIFTEEN

(1) *Viaggio*, p. 172.

(2) *Ibid.*, pp. 177-8.

(3) *Ibid.*, p. 179.

(4) *Ibid.*, p. 195.

(5) *Ibid.*, pp. 201-2.

(6) *Ibid.*, pp. 200-1.

(7) *Ibid.*, p. 213.

(8) *Ibid.*, p. 222.

(9) *Ibid.*, p. 218.

(10) *Ibid.*, pp. 219-20.

(11) *Ibid.*, p. 247.

(12) *The Pylgrymage of Sir Richard Guylforde*, pp. 82-3.

(13) *Viaggio*, p. 262.

(14) *Ibid.*, p. 267.

(15) *Ibid.*, p. 285.

Notes

(1) *Viaggio*, p. 189. This event caused them surprise as well as joy. See Mitchell: *The Laurels and the Tiara*, pp. 127-8.

(2) Aeneas Sylvius Piccolomini: *Commentarii*, Book I, Frankfurt, 1614.

(3) *Viaggio*, p. 300.

(4) *Ibid.*, pp. 311-12.

(5) *Ibid.*, p. 313.

(6) As we know from an oration he made before the Doge. This is to be found in a XV-century MS. in the Bibliothèque Nationale, Paris, MS. 8130, ff. 30-4.

(7) E. Motta: *Gian Giacomo Trivulzio in Terra Santa*, *1476*.

(8) *Viaggio*, p. 315.

(9) Roberto gives a long list (*Viaggio*, p. 317) that includes Antonio Capodilista, Auditor of Cardinal Scarampo, who must have returned from Rome very recently. See p. 170.

(10) *Viaggio*, p. 323.

(11) *Ibid.*, p. 326.

INDEX

Adrianople, 22

Alberto, Francesco di, 56, 165, 168, 171-3

Alexandria, Milanese envoys to, 23

Alfonso, King of Aragon and Naples, 71, 162, 171

Arimathea, 99

Balestrieri, 61

Balm, Garden of (balsam), 149-50

Barbo, Niccolò, 72n., 73

Beirut, 126-8

Belbeis, 159

Beltramo, Alvise, 128, 165, 169

Bethlehem, 112-17, 161

Blackader, Robert, 85n.

Bochatij, David de, 68

Bosso, Carlo, 34, 109-11, 112-13, 119

Brasca, Santo, 17, 196

Brenner Pass, 45, 122

Butigella, Conradino, 34, 180

Butigella, Giovanni Matteo, 34-5, 189

    mission to Alexandria, 23n., 35

    knighted in Jerusalem, 109-11

    stays on in Jerusalem, 119, 135

    tends Martino, 131-2

    writes Historia Jerosolomitana, 135

    meets Sanseverino in Bethlehem, 161

    returns to Milan with Sanseverino (q.v.), 163ff.

Butigella, Giovanni Stefano, 135

Cairo, 151ff.

Calcenoni, Domenico da, 36, 112

Calistano, Antonio, 131n., 167

Calixtus III, Pope, 175

Caloyers, 147

Candia, 73

Capodilista, Antonio 40

    at Candia, 73

    in Rhodes, 76ff.

    in Jerusalem, 100

    to Bethlehem, 113

    sails for home, 119

    reaches home, 121

    at Mello, 170

Capodilista, Francesco, 40, 180-1

Capodilista, Gabriele, 40-1, 75-6, 181, 188

    starts from Padua, 41

    at Ragusa, 68-9

    at Candia, 73

    in Rhodes, 76ff.

    in Cyprus, 85, 119-20

    in Jerusalem, 100-3

    sails for home, 119

    reaches home, 121-2

Cardona, Giovanni di, 170

Casola, Pietro, 103, 106

Castiglione, Cardinal Giovanni, 176-7

Catering on board ship, 62-3, 81, 166-7, 169

Cattaveri, the, 48, 58

Chanico, 159

Chioggia, 38, 50, 179

Coeur, Jacques, 126

Compostella, 22, 65

Constantinople, capture of, 21, 28

Contarini, Alessandro, 71-2

Contracts for voyage, 19, 53-4, 86

Copts, 26 & n.

Cornaro, Andrea, 83-5, 120, 171

Crispi, Giovanni, 169

Index

Crusades, 16
Cyprus, 83-5, 119-20

Damascus, 125-7
Debbet-el-Ramla, 142
Decembrio, Angelo, 35, 132
Decembrio, Pier Candido, 35
Derby, Henry, Earl of, 64, 118
Diano, Rosso da, 175, 177-8
Diedo, Baldessare, 58, 62, 63, 64,
    70-1, 87, 119
Donato, Fra, 136n.
Drella, Giovanni Antonio, 132, 167,
    179
Durazzo, 71

Emmaus, 99
Episkopi, 83-5
Eustachio, Fenone degli, 37, 112

Fabri, Felix, 92, 104, 147, 202, 205
Falasco, Baldessare, 173-4
Ferrante, King of Naples, 162, 171
Figarolo, battle of, 129, 156n.
Fogliano, Corrado da, 23n., 30, 35,
    183
Fondaco dei Tedeschi, 47
Food, see Catering
Francesco, Fra, 100, 134, 137, 145,
    148, 163
Franco, Antonio di, 133, 140-1

Gabriele, D. Jeronimo, 165n.
Galeotti, 55-6, 61-2, 77, 86, 125
Galleys, Venetian, 52, 54ff.
    licensing of, 54, 124
    and see Loredana
Gaza (Gazara), 137, 160
Gazelus, the, 133
Gentili, Hilario, 112
Glusiano, Giovanni da, 37
Gonzaga, Lodovico, 183
Guiniforte of Piacenza, 132, 167

Guylforde, Sir Richard, 102

Helena, Queen of Cyprus, 85
Helena, Saint and Empress, 107, 144
Historia Jerosolomitana, 135, 189
Holy Sepulchre, Church of, 99-100,
    104-11
    Knights of, 109
Hurlegh, John, 108

*Information for Pilgrims unto the
    Holy Land*, 19, 49, 51, 115
    190
Itineraries of William Wey, the,
    19-21, 44-6, 93-4, 116-17, 190
Itinerario in Terra Santa (Capo-
    dilista), 41, 66, 105, 122, 188

Jacomo (interpreter), 137, 140, 143
Jaffa, 87
    landing formalities, 88-90
    stampede for donkeys, 90-2
Jerusalem, 99ff., 132, 136, 161-3
John II, King of Cyprus, 85, 120
John of Prussia, Brother, 110
Jordan, river, 116

Kanis, 159
Katiyeh, 160
Kempe, Margery, 17, 105, 202

Larkes, Master, 19, 115, 190
Leza, the, 127-9
Limasol, 83-4
Lodi, peace of, 22
Loredan, Antonio, 54-5, 58, 87,
    101, 119
    business in Damascus, 125ff., 163
    charters *Leza* for return, 127, 165
    charged with fraud in Venice, 128
    fights under Sanseverino, 129
    death, 129
Loredan, Niccolò, 55, 87, 89

Index

Loredana, the, 54-5, 58
  accommodation and crew, 60-2
  catering, 62-3, 81
  her companion galley, 64
  sails for home, 119
  reaches Venice, 121
Loreto, Our Lady of, 168, 173, 176-7
Lydda, 97

Mahomet (guide), 101, 132, 137, 140, 151-3
Mahomet II, Sultan, 21, 27, 121
Malatesta, Sigismondo, 178
Malavolti, Lucrezia, 32n., 183n.
Malvezzi, Lodovico, 182
Mamluks, 24, 153-7, 159
Maripietro, Pasquale, 53n.
Martino de Ferrariis, Giovanni, 33, 119
  ill in Jerusalem, 127, 131
  recovers, 135, 161-2
  stays on at Mount Syon, 163
Martino Tedesco, 33, 132, 167
Matariya, 149-51, 159
Maxentius, Emperor, 144
Mello, 169-71
Messa Secca, 67
Milan, Duchy of, 23, 30
Modone, 171-2
Montefeltro, Federigo da, 178-9
Mount Syon, 101, 163
  Franciscan Brothers, 100, 104, 131, 132, 134
Muffel, Gabriel, 43, 146
Muslims, 24-8, 105-6, 138
  use of term, 24n.
  pilgrims' attitude to, 28, 93, 157, 164
  and see Saracens, Turks

Nicholas of Cusa, Cardinal, 27

Nicopolis, battle of, 21

Patrono, 54-5, 86-7
Pelchinger, Anton, 64, 189
Pia, Marquis Carlo, 178
Piccinino, Jacopo, 31n.
Piccinino, Niccolò, 31n.
Piccolomini, Aeneas Sylvius, 21, 22, 175, 200
  and see Pius II
Pilgrim Book (Muffel), 43, 146
Pilgrimage, 15ff
  licence for, 21, 35, 46, 158
Pilgrims, numbers of, 22
  information and advice for, 18-21, 48-9, 93-4, 96-7
  guide-books for, 18-21
  the Milanese party, 30ff.
  the Paduan party, 39ff.
  the English party, 42-6
  deaths of, 85-6
  as souvenir hunters, 94, 118
Pius II, Pope, 21, 27, 28, 171, 177
Pormano, Jacopo, 38
Provisions, 133
  and see Catering
Pusterlo, Pietro, 35n.

Quarantana, Mount, 116

Ragusa, 68-9
Ramleh, 92, 97-8
Rhodes, 73, 76ff., 120-1
  Knights of, 78
  Hospital, 79
  Arsenal, 79, 81
Riva, Gaspare da, 171

St. Catherine of Alexandria, 144-5
  shrine of, 144, 146-7
St. Gotthard Pass, 45
Saladin, 155-6
Sanseverino, Francesco da, 182

Index

Sanseverino, Contessa Johanna, 183
Sanseverino, Roberto da, 23, 187-8
  on Copts, 26n.
  earlier career, 30-2
  portraits of, 32
  starts from Milan, 36
  arrives in Venice, 39
  visits the Doge, 53-4
  boards his galley, 58
  at Ragusa, 68-9
  in Adriatic gale, 70
  at Durazzo, 72
  at Candia, 73
  escapes from pirate ship, 74
  in Rhodes, 77ff.
  at Ramleh, 97-8
  at Jerusalem, 99ff., 132
  provisions for Sinai journey, 133-4
  at Sinai, 143ff.
  in Cairo, 152ff.
  visits the Sultan, 155-7
  leaves for Jerusalem, 159
  arrives at Jerusalem, 161
  to Acre, 164
  sails for home, 166
  at Mello, 170
  lands at Ancona, 173-4
  arrives Venice overland, 180
  reaches Milan, 183
  death, 31, 184
Santa Maria di Artone, 168, 182
Saracens, 24-6, 93, 164
  and see Muslims, Turks
Scarampo, Cardinal Luigi, 76, 170
Schiavo, Marco, 167
Sfondrati, Bartolomeo di, 68-9
Sforza, Alessandro, 56
Sforza, Duke Francesco, 23, 30, 33, 35, 175, 179
Sforza, Galeazzo, 183
Sigoli, Simone, 158
Sinai, Mount, 141, 144ff.
  Brethren at, 134, 143, 145, 147

Solomon's Pools, 137
Souvenirs, 94, 118
Superantio, Marco, 128
Syon, Mount, see Mount Syon

Tafur, Pero, 83, 102, 120, 131, 134, 197, 200, 203
Tholomarii, the, 48-9
Tiptoft, John, Earl of Worcester, 187
  earlier and later career, 42-4, 121
  arrives in Venice, 58
  in Rhodes, 77ff.
  in Jerusalem, 108
  performs knighting ceremony, 109-10
  to Bethlehem, 113
  sails for Venice, 119
  studies at Padua, 122
Tomaso, 85
Tragorino, Antonio, 171
Trivulzio, Gian Giacomo, 180-1
Trono, Jacomo, 173, 176, 178, 180
Turks, Ottoman, 21-4
  capture Constantinople, 21, 28
  advance into Morea, 71
  hostility to Rhodes, 121
  and see Muslims, Saracens

Valturio, Roberto, 156
Varese, Marquis of, 39
Varna, battle, of, 22
Venice, 47ff.
  facilities for pilgrims' will-making, 16
  and pilgrim traffic, 23, 53
  trade with London, 44
  trade with the East, 126-7
  inns, 47-8
  shops, 49-51
  Arsenal, 51-2

Index

Viaggio in Terra Santa (San-severino), 30, 32, 66, 103, 187-8
quoted, *passim*
Vinterio, Brother, 115
Visconti, Bianca, 34 & n.
Vitry, Jacques de, 135

Walther, Brother Paul, 27n.
Wedding of the Sea, 56-7

Wey, William, 44-6, 64
his *Itineraries*, 19-21, 96-7 *et passim*
his map, 19-20
on Saracens, 25
acquires souvenirs, 94-5
preaches in Jerusalem, 108
sails for home, 119
later life, 123
Worcester, Earl of, *see* Tiptoft, John